UCHICAGO Consortium on School Research

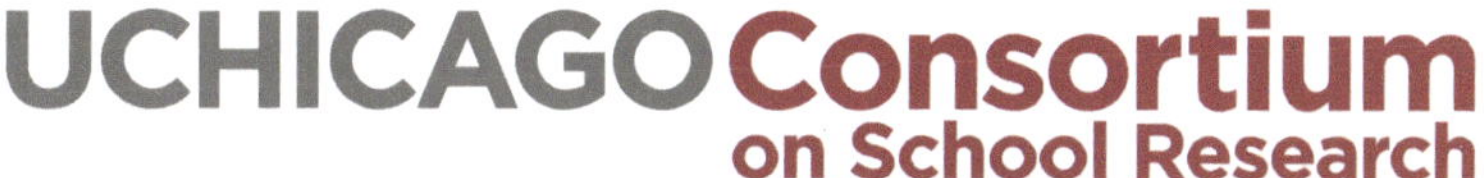

RESEARCH REPORT JUNE 2020

Trends in Computer Science Education

Access, Enrollment, and Performance in CPS High Schools

Lisa Barrow, Silvana Freire, and Marisa de la Torre

TABLE OF CONTENTS

ACKNOWLEDGEMENTS

The authors wish to acknowledge the many people who have contributed to this study, especially those who provided much appreciated feedback and constructive criticism. At Chicago Public Schools, Sarah Dickson and the Office of Computer Science have been great partners in this work. In particular, Lucia Dettori and Andrew Rasmussen answered data questions, helped us to better understand the different initiatives that the district has undertaken to expand access to and participation in Computer Science across the city, and provided helpful feedback at different stages of the project. Additionally, we would like to extend our thanks to Steven McGee for generously giving us some of his time and sharing his expertise.

Before we started writing this report, we presented preliminary findings to members of our Steering Committee, who provided helpful feedback and suggestions to improve our analysis, interpretation, and subsequent writing. Additionally, we received written feedback on the final draft from Steering Committee members Nancy Lee Chavez and Paige Ponder, and thank them for their thorough and thoughtful comments.

We appreciate the contributions of our Consortium colleagues who read multiple drafts of this report and provided us with valuable suggestions for improvement, including John Easton, Elaine Allensworth, Alyssa Blanchard, and Jessica Tansey. We thank our colleague Todd Rosenkranz, who conducted a thorough technical read of the report and the UChicago Consortium's communications team, including Jessica Tansey, Jessica Puller, Alida Mitau, and Lisa Sall who were instrumental in the production of this report. We also appreciate the help of Consortium research assistants Paloma Blandon, Grace Su, Tala Ali-Hasan, Sarthak Panwar, and Baunnee Martinez who performed literature reviews, helped systematize and synthesize data, and undertook edits of the report. Additionally, we would like to acknowledge Jennie Jiang, Elizabeth Frank, Gonzalo Pons, and Andrew Zou who collaborated in the initial stage of this project.

We are grateful for funding from the CME Group Foundation which supported this work by providing time and resources to conduct the analyses and write the report. The UChicago Consortium greatly appreciates support from the Consortium Investor Council that funds critical work beyond the initial research: putting the research to work, refreshing the data archive, seeding new studies, and replicating previous studies. Members include: Brinson Family Foundation, CME Group Foundation, Crown Family Philanthropies, Lloyd A. Fry Foundation, Joyce Foundation, Lewis-Sebring Family Foundation, McCormick Foundation, McDougal Family Foundation, Osa Family Foundation, Polk Bros. Foundation, Spencer Foundation, Steans Family Foundation, and The Chicago Public Education Fund. We also extend our thanks for the operating grants provided by the Spencer Foundation and the Lewis-Sebring Family Foundation, which support the work of the UChicago Consortium.

Cite as: Barrow, L., Freire, S., & de la Torre, M. (2020). *Trends in computer science education: Access, enrollment, and performance in CPS High Schools.* Chicago, IL: University of Chicago Consortium on School Research.

This report was produced by the UChicago Consortium's publications and communications staff : Lisa Sall, Director of Outreach and Communication; Jessica Tansey, Communications Manager; Jessica Puller, Communications Specialist; and Alida Mitau, Development and Communications Coordinator.

Graphic Design: Jeff Hall Design
Photography: Eileen Ryan
Editing: Jessica Tansey and Jessica Puller

06.2020/PDF/jh.design@rcn.com

Executive Summary

The last several years have seen high-profile efforts by districts, states, not-for-profit organizations, and the federal government to expand Computer Science (CS) education in K–12 schools in the United States. Beyond simply expanding CS offerings at the K–12 level, these efforts have included adopting curricula and policies with the specific goal of increasing the diversity of students with exposure to CS. In the longer-run, the hope is to create a more diverse technology workforce and a more inclusive and collaborative culture within the industry.

Chicago Public Schools (CPS) was an early leader in K–12 CS expansion; the district unveiled its CS4All plan in 2013, aimed at exposing students to CS concepts from kindergarten through twelfth grade and providing them with 21st century content and skills to thrive in today's digital economy. The policy involved the adoption of a curriculum and professional development program known as Exploring Computer Science (ECS) that was designed to be accessible to all students and to broaden participation in CS. The CPS policy also included a plan to make CS a graduation requirement, making CPS the first school district in the country to adopt such a policy. The graduating class of 2020 (ninth-grade cohort 2016–17) is the first cohort of students subject to this requirement.

After the 2013 announcement of Chicago's CS4All initiative, other large cities like New York and San Francisco adopted similar plans, and in 2016 President Obama announced CS4All as a nationwide initiative that built on the CS4All work in Chicago and in other states and localities. This study presents a first look at CPS's efforts to make CS education more accessible and meaningful to all students, focusing on the recent CPS changes aimed at increasing participation in CS among high school students. Efforts to increase exposure at all grade levels is ongoing, and a more complete picture will become available when today's elementary school students ultimately graduate from high school.

Specifically, this study examines trends in CS education[1] in Chicago over the last decade in CPS high schools.[2] This longitudinal look describes the state of CS in CPS 10 years ago, what progress has been made by the district, and what challenges still remain to be addressed. We utilize data from 2008–09 through 2017–18 and explore these questions through three components: CS access, enrollment, and performance. We examine these three components before and after the adoption of the ECS curriculum, and examine differences by gender, race/ethnicity, and neighborhood socioeconomic status (SES). We look specifically at the cohorts of students who will graduate under the new CS graduation requirement in 2020 and 2021, but note that our data are incomplete for these cohorts and thus findings are preliminary.

---

1 See *What is Computer Science?* on p.5 for a brief explanation of the concept of CS education and clarification about some common misconceptions around this academic field.

2 Charter high schools were excluded from our analyses because our data archive currently does not include records of charter school students' transcripts. Additionally, non-traditional high schools within CPS, such as Options Schools and special education schools, were excluded from our analyses because of differences in their course requirements for students.

Key Findings

Access to CS increased steadily following the announcement of the CS4All initiative; by 2018, more than 90 percent of students attending CPS high schools were enrolled in a high school that offered at least one CS course. And 80 percent of CPS high schools offered at least one CS course by 2018. Across the city, more than 60 percent of high schools in each geographic region were offering CS. High schools not yet offering a CS course were mostly located in neighborhoods on the South and West Sides of the city. The majority of the increase in high schools offering CS followed the announcement of the CS4All initiative in December 2013, and that increase was mainly driven by an expansion in the number of schools offering at least one introductory-level CS course, most using the ECS curriculum. Because larger high schools were the most likely to offer CS, 92 percent of high school students in 2018 were enrolled in a school that offered at least one CS course. This was up from 52 percent of high school students in 2009. CPS reports that all district-run high schools are offering CS in the 2019–20 school year.[3]

Annual enrollment in CS increased steadily following the introduction of ECS in the 2012–13 school year, especially in introductory-level courses. Cohort enrollment rates also increased over time, with particularly large increases for the cohorts subject to the new CS graduation requirement. Only 8 percent of the 2010–11 cohort took at least one CS course after four years of high school, compared with 26 percent of the 2014–15 cohort. Increases in ninth-grade enrollment rates primarily drove the increases at the cohort level. Ninth-grade enrollment rates increased even more sharply among cohorts subject to the graduation requirement (who had not yet completed four years of school at the time of this report). In only one year of high school, cohort enrollment rates for those subject to the graduation requirement exceeded the cohort enrollment rates over four years of high school for those not subject to the graduation requirement.

While Asian students remained more likely to enroll in a CS course than other students in the district, enrollment rates increased for all race/ethnicity groups. Differences in enrollment rates by race/ethnicity and neighborhood SES at the district level were due in part to differences in access to CS courses. Black students were the least likely overall to enroll in a CS course, in part because they were the least likely to attend a school that offered CS. Once we account for differences in access to CS, Black students were the most likely to enroll in a CS course. Asian students were also more likely than average to enroll in a CS course, even after accounting for access, while Latino and White students were somewhat less likely than average to enroll in a CS course.

Students living in the lowest-SES neighborhoods were 3 percentage points less likely to enroll in a CS course, relative to the overall average. This difference was largely due to these students being less likely to attend a high school that offered a CS course. Once we account for differences in access to CS courses, students living in the lowest-SES neighborhoods were about as likely as the average student to enroll in a CS course.

Enrollment rates increased for both male and female students, but male students were more likely to enroll in a CS course than female students, even within schools offering CS. Given that female students were somewhat more likely to attend a school that offered CS, this difference widens when we account for access to CS. Further, this enrollment rate difference widened after the introduction of the ECS curriculum. Although enrollment rates for both male and female students increased after the introduction and expansion of ECS courses, the increase was faster for male students. For the cohort of first-time ninth-graders in 2014–15 (the most recent cohort in our sample to have completed four years of high school), 30 percent of male students took at least one CS course over their first four years of high school, compared with 21 percent of female students in the cohort, a difference of 9 percentage

---

3 See CPS Office of Computer Science website, "Where Can My Child Take Computer Science" https://sites.google.com/cps. edu/cs4all/for-parents/where-can-my-child-take-cs

points. This was up from a difference of 4 percentage points in the 2010–11 cohort and 3 percentage points in the 2008–09 cohort.

Overall and across student groups, students earned higher average grades in CS courses than in core courses, and few students failed CS courses. Across cohorts, average CS grades exceeded students' grade averages in core courses by about 0.2 grade points. These differences in average grades were similar across gender, race/ethnicity, and neighborhood SES groups. In 2018, almost 70 percent of the grades earned in CS classes were As or Bs, and only 4 percent were failing grades. Because few students failed a CS course, increased enrollment in CS courses translated into increases in the share of students earning at least one CS credit. Twenty-one percent of students in the 2014–15 cohort who graduated in 2018 earned at least one credit in CS.

Implications

CPS has been at the forefront of making computer science an integral part of students' education from kindergarten through twelfth grade. With the introduction of a new curriculum and professional development, the expansion of the number of high schools offering CS classes, and the CS graduation requirement, more students gained exposure to computer science in their schools. We will begin to see the full impact of these efforts as more student cohorts graduate with the CS course requirement.

As many districts across the nation are adding CS to their curriculum at both the elementary and high school levels, this study presents what one school district has done to increase CS education, and some of the successes and challenges they faced. Our findings offer important considerations for CPS and other districts expanding their CS offerings:

1. **Access:** After the introduction of CS4All, CPS rapidly expanded CS offerings at the high school level. While some smaller schools had yet to offer CS courses when the first cohorts subject to the graduation requirement initially entered high school, CPS reports that all CPS high schools offered at least one CS course in the 2019–20 school year. Recruiting, training, and retaining skilled teachers may be one of the main challenges to address for any district looking to provide universal CS access. These challenges are likely to be particularly prevalent in high schools that face difficulties in staffing teachers due to small overall enrollment or shortages of teachers in particular areas of study. The difficulty in staffing teachers who can teach Advanced Placement (AP) CS courses is even more acute; these teachers typically require certification in math, technology, or computer science (depending on the AP course), in addition to AP professional development, and nationwide the number of teachers certified in these areas is small. Districts may want to evaluate their CS teacher pipelines and develop specific strategies to staff CS courses.

2. **Enrollment:** While CS is now a graduation requirement in CPS, district guidelines allow some students to receive waivers for the requirement.[4] The ability of students to obtain CS waivers will have implications for the CS enrollment capacity needed by each high school. Waivers may also affect whether differences in CS enrollment rates persist. In particular, female students were less likely than their male peers to enroll in CS as an elective, and this enrollment difference was not due to differential access to CS courses. If waiver-eligible female students are more likely than waiver-eligible male students to take up a waiver, then some difference in enrollment rates between male and female students may persist. Districts focused on engaging female students in CS content and courses may want to track enrollment rates, consider their students' experiences, and address potential barriers to engagement.

3. **Graduation Requirement:** Especially in early years of implementation, course availability is a logistical hurdle for districts and schools to address. Less than one-half of the students in the first CPS cohort with the CS graduation requirement (the 2016–17 cohort) had earned at least one CS credit at the end of their

---

4 See *Computer Science in CPS* p.7 for more information about requirements and waivers.

second year of high school. Though some of these students may be eligible for and ultimately utilize waivers, that may not be true for all students. Thus, high school administrators will need to be closely tracking access (e.g., seats available, class scheduling, staffing needs, etc.) to ensure all students who need to enroll in CS courses can do so. Districts likely want to account and solve for key logistical details when implementing new CS graduation requirements.

Introduction

The last several years have seen high-profile efforts by districts, states, and not-for-profit organizations to expand Computer Science (CS) education in K–12 schools in the United States. At the federal level, President Obama's 2016 budget proposal included four billion dollars for state grants and 100 million dollars for district grants for Computer Science for All (CS4All) plans.[5]

State-level efforts included adopting state K–12 CS standards, policies requiring all high schools to offer CS courses, and policies allowing a CS course to count as a core graduation credit.[6] Closer to home, Chicago Public Schools (CPS) unveiled its CS4All plan in 2013 with the goals of offering CS curriculum in 25 percent of all elementary schools and every public high school, an Advanced Placement (AP) CS course in one-half of all high schools, and making CS a high school graduation requirement.[7] It was the first district in the country to require students to complete a CS course in order to graduate.[8]

Behind this effort to ensure students take a CS course is the idea that, in today's economy, everyone needs CS to go beyond just being a consumer of technology to being able to use technology and computational thinking to solve problems. Computational thinking is described as a set of skills that typically include recognizing patterns and sequences, creating algorithms, devising strategies for finding and fixing errors, reducing the general to the precise, and expanding the precise to the general.[9] These skills have many applications in a wide range of areas and industries. As such, a basic education in CS is considered essential in the 21st century in the same way that schools provide a basic education in biology and other core subjects.

Computers and computational thinking are essential skills for jobs that are in high-demand. Nearly one-half of STEM occupations are related to computers, and employment in computer and information technology occupations is projected to increase by 13 percent between 2016 and 2026, compared with 7 percent growth for all occupations.[10] In addition, computer and information technology occupations are among the highest paid, with a median annual wage around $86,000 as of May 2018. Yet, the current number of graduates from CS college programs will not be able to meet the projected demand.

What is Computer Science?

Despite a clear recognition of the importance of computer science education, many relevant stakeholders—students, parents, teachers and school administrators—are not able to accurately distinguish between the general use of computers (i.e., computer literacy) and computer science. In particular, one of the most common misconceptions around computer science is

---

5 Heitin (2016, January 30).
6 Code.org Advocacy Coalition (2019); Google Inc., & Gallup Inc. (2017).
7 Goode & Margolis (2011); Reed, Wilkerson, Yanek, Dettori, & Solin (2015); Zumbach (2013, December 10).
8 Elahi (2016, March 1).
9 Papanno (2017, April 4).
10 Fayer, Lacey, & Watson (2017); Bureau of Labor Statistics (2019). The Bureau of Labor Statistics data do not distinguish between computer science and information technology occupations.

that it includes the creation of digital documents and presentations and the use of the Internet.[11] However, what is taught in a CS course involves critical thinking, collaboration, and encouraging students to be active producers and creators of new technologies instead of passive users of existing technologies.

To inform the creation of K–12 CS curricula, several school districts and states have followed the framework proposed by the Association for Computing Machinery taskforce, which defines computer science as "the study of computers and algorithmic processes, including their principles, their hardware and software designs, their implementation, and their impact on society." [12] As such, the field of computer science goes far beyond learning how to code in a specific programming language. It involves the collection, storage, and analysis of data and focuses on developing computational skills to solve complex problems, designing computing applications, and understanding the social implications of these new technologies.[13]

By drawing on the fundamental concepts of computer science, computational thinking entails formulating problems and solutions, designing systems, and understanding human behavior.[14] This approach to solving complex problems involves strategies such as breaking a problem into parts (decomposition), finding similarities and differences between the parts (pattern recognition), finding the general principles behind these patterns (abstraction), and developing step-by-step instructions to solve similar problems (algorithm design). Students would be using computational thinking skills if, for example, instead of just entering data into a spreadsheet to create a chart, they generated algorithms to automate the transformation of the data.[15]

Additionally, foundational principles of CS intersect with math, science, and engineering concepts. For instance, mathematical and scientific thinking involves developing computational thinking skills and using abstractions to create models and artifacts to solve problems.[16] Similarly, CS draws on engineering thinking when designing and building systems that interact with the real world.[17]

Although CS builds on other computer-related areas, these areas have distinctive characteristics that differentiate them from CS itself, as they mainly focus on using computer technologies rather than understanding why and how they work. These related areas include:[18]

- **Computer Literacy:** General use of computers and programs (e.g., creating digital presentations).

- **Educational Technology:** Applying computer literacy in different school subjects (e.g., students in English class using web-based applications to aid their learning).

- **Digital Citizenship:** Appropriate and responsible use of technology (e.g., choosing an appropriately secure password).

- **Information Technology:** Industrial application of CS (e.g., installing software rather than creating it).

Computer Science Education

CS is a well-developed program of study at the college and university level. Nearly every college or university offers a CS major. In contrast, CS is much less prevalent at the elementary and secondary school levels. A 2016 Google-Gallup survey on K–12 trends in CS found that only 60 percent of K–12 principals (78 percent of high school principals) reported having at least one CS course available at their schools.[19] This is likely an overstatement of the prevalence of course offerings, as many may mistake offering courses in applications that use computers (e.g., keyboarding, word processors) with offering a CS course. Among schools that did not report offering any CS courses, principals identified several barriers to offering CS—a shortage of teachers with the necessary skills, not enough money to hire or train a teacher, and the need to focus on courses related to tested subjects (i.e., those used for accountability systems). [20]

11 Google Inc., & Gallup Inc. (2015).
12 Tucker, McCowan, Deek, Stephenson, Jones, & Verno (2006).
13 Association for Computing Machinery (ACM) (2016).
14 Wing (2006).
15 ACM (2016).

16 ACM (2016).
17 Wing (2006).
18 ACM (2016).
19 Google Inc., & Gallup Inc. (2016).
20 Yadav, Gretter, Hambrusch, & Sands (2016).

Equity of access to and participation in CS, both at the college and high school levels, has received much recent attention. The latest report on the state of CS education indicates that less than one-half of high schools nationwide teach computer science.[21] Across the 39 states participating in the study, high schools in rural areas, those with higher percentages of underrepresented minority students, and those with higher percentages of students eligible for free or reduced-price lunch were less likely to offer CS courses. In addition, female, Black, and Latino students are underrepresented in the field at both the high school and college level. In 2016, 81 percent of undergraduate degrees in CS were awarded to men, and a slightly lower percentage (71 percent) of students sitting for the 2019 AP Computer Science exam (Computer Science A or Computer Science Principles) were male.[22] Black and Latino students represented only 6 and 17 percent of AP CS exam takers nationwide, respectively.[23, 24] Similarly, a recent study on the state of CS education in California found significant disparities in terms of CS access and participation at the high school level by race/ethnicity, gender, and SES. For instance, while only 39 percent of high schools were offering CS courses, schools predominantly serving Black, Latino, and/or Native American students were nearly half as likely to offer any CS course. Less than one-third of students who enrolled in an introductory CS courses or took the AP CS A exam were female; among AP CS A test-takers, only 16 percent were Black, Latino, or Native American—which comprise 60 percent of California's high school population.[25]

Computer Science in CPS

Prior to the 2011–12 school year, computer science had little central organization within CPS. Some high schools offered a variety of CS and IT courses, but there was minimal standardization across schools. Many computer-oriented courses were primarily about learning basic word-processing, spreadsheet skills, and using the Internet. The CS courses offered included introductory CS courses, specific language programming courses, network and web design, and AP CS courses.[26]

In 2009, CPS began revamping the curriculum for the Career and Technical Education (CTE) programs, which typically included CS courses. As part of that task, in 2011, CPS partnered with the Computer Science Teachers Association (CSTA), The Learning Partnership, and faculty from DePaul, Loyola, and the University of Illinois at Chicago to adapt and introduce a new curriculum known as Exploring Computer Science (ECS) into one of the Information Technology CTE tracks.[27, 28] ECS was attractive to CPS both because it could be adapted to fit the needs of the CTE program and because it was designed to be inclusive and accessible to all students. A major goal of ECS was to broaden participation in CS among women and other student groups who are traditionally underrepresented in CS by providing inquiry-based and culturally-relevant instruction. Additionally, the ECS professional development (PD) attempts to change teachers and counselors' stereotypes and beliefs about who is likely to succeed in CS. The hope is that these efforts will create a more inclusive learning environment in which all students gain an understanding of computer science and problem solving as well as exposure to many real-world applications of computer science.[29]

ECS implementation in CPS began in the 2012–13 school year as a high school introductory-level CS course.[30] One important component of adopting the ECS curriculum was providing PD to teachers.[31] By fall 2013, 75 teachers had been trained through the ECS PD program.

---

21 Code.org Advocacy Coalition (2019).

22 Snyder, de Brey, & Dillow (2019); The College Board (2019).

23 The College Board (2019).

24 For comparison, the U.S. Department of Education National Center for Education Statistics projected that 14 percent of high school graduates in 2018–19 would be Black and 23 percent would be Hispanic/Latino. See NCES (2018) for more details.

25 Scott et al. (2019).

26 For examples and a more detailed description of CS courses currently offered at CPS high schools see Table A.1. in Appendix A.

27 See Century et al. (2013) for a more comprehensive description of the CPS and Chicago CSTA history.

28 Reed et al. (2015).

29 Margolis, Ryoo, Sandoval, Lee, Goode, & Chapman (2012).

30 The ECS curriculum is used in different introductory-level CS courses within CPS, such as Exploring Computer Science, Fundamentals of IT, STEM Intro to Computer Science, and Taste of Computing.

31 The ECS teacher PD involves a five-day summer PD session followed by one year of teaching combined with mini-PD sessions during the school year and a second five-day PD session the following summer.

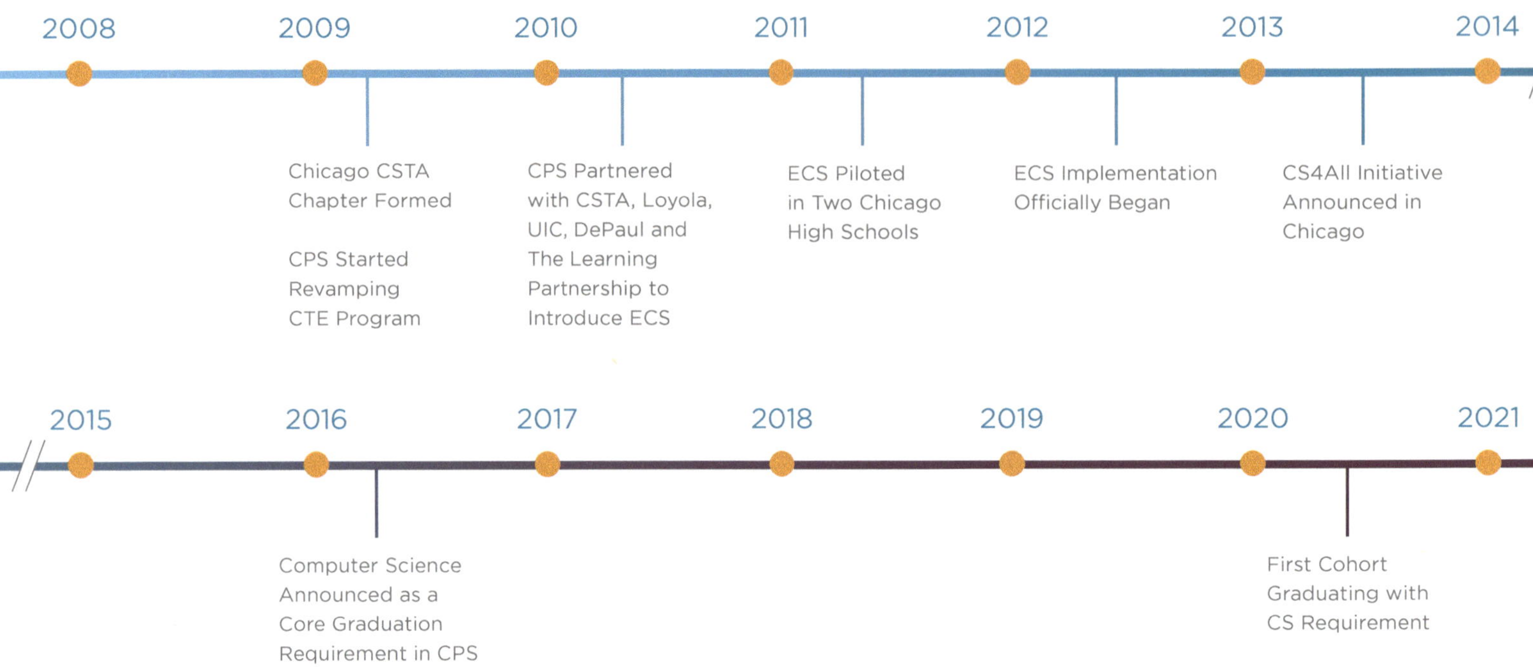

More backing for expanding CS came in December 2013 with the announcement of the CPS CS4All initiative. The five-year plan included several goals: offering the new ECS curriculum in every CPS high school, offering CS curriculum in 25 percent of all elementary schools, offering an AP CS course in one-half of all high schools, and making CS a high school graduation requirement.[32] Indeed, in February 2016, CPS became the first school district in the nation to make CS a core graduation requirement beginning with the high school cohort set to graduate in 2020.[33]

In order to add CS as a core graduation requirement, CPS modified the existing credit-bearing graduation requirements, from two credits in Career Education to one credit in Career Education and one credit in CS. Compared to the CS graduation requirement, the Career Education requirement is more flexible, as there are courses across many subject areas that can fulfill it. For example, Multivariable Calculus, Carpentry I, and Composition & Rhetoric all satisfy the Career Education credit requirement.[34] In contrast, courses satisfying the CS requirement (based on the high school course catalog) are all courses in CS. However, some students will be eligible to receive waivers for the CS requirement. In particular, International Baccalaureate (IB) students in either the IB Diploma Programme or the IB Career-related Programme, CTE students who "will have taken two courses in a single CTE pathway by the end of junior year," and students pursuing advanced coursework required by a college or university are eligible to receive a waiver for the CS graduation requirement.[35]

---

32 Reed et al. (2015); Zumbach (2013, December 10).
33 Elahi (2016, March 10).
34 CPS Office of Teaching and Learning (2019).
35 CPS Office of Computer Science (n.d.).

This Study

As Chicago students begin to graduate with CS course requirements and interest in CS education grows nationwide, it is important to understand the opportunities offered to students in terms of CS. Prior studies in Chicago have focused on the effectiveness of the ECS curriculum, examining the degree to which enrolling in an ECS course influences students' engagement and participation in computer science.[36] Yet, it is not known whether and to what extent these initiatives led to broader changes in the landscape of CS education in Chicago. Namely, if they led students to take and succeed in CS courses and/or if they decreased inequalities in access, enrollment, and performance in CS.

In this report, we aim to answer these questions by taking a longitudinal look at CPS's efforts to expand CS education at the high school level. We also examine student enrollment and performance in CS courses and explore changes in differences by students' gender, race/ethnicity, and SES. In particular, we use data on CPS high schools from school years 2008–09 through 2017–18 to answer the following research questions:

- How did CS offerings change over time, and did CS offerings differ by school characteristics?
- How did student enrollment in CS change over time?
  - Were there differences in CS course-taking by student characteristics?
  - Were these enrollment differences related to differences in access to CS?
- How well did students perform in CS courses?
  - What grades did students receive in their CS classes?
  - How many CS credits were students earning?
  - How did students' grades in CS compare to their grades in other subject areas?
  - Did differences between CS and core course grades vary by gender, race/ethnicity, and/or neighborhood SES?

Chapter 1 explores access to CS courses across CPS high schools, and **Chapter 2** investigates which students enrolled in these courses. **Chapter 3** examines students' performance in CS courses and how they compare to other courses. **Chapter 4** describes implications of the findings.

---

36 McGee et al. (2018, April 14); McGee et al. (2017); Dettori, Greenburg, McGee, & Reed (2016).

Access to Computer Science

Key Takeaways on CS Access

- **The number of schools offering at least one CS course increased over the study period**, with the largest gains following the announcement of the CS4All initiative in December 2013. In 2018, 90 percent of students were attending a school that offered a CS course.

- **Expansion of access** was geographically widespread, and by 2018, more than 60 percent of CPS high schools in each geographic region of the city were offering at least one CS course.

- **Twenty percent of CPS high schools did not yet offer any CS courses in 2018.** All selective enrollment high schools offered at least one CS course; schools that did not have a course typically had lower student enrollment.

This chapter describes the expansion of CS course offerings in CPS from 2008–09 through 2017–18. In particular, it examines how offerings of any CS course, as well as specific levels or types of CS courses—introductory, intermediate, and AP—changed over time. It also describes which school characteristics were related to CS offerings before and after the introduction of the ECS curriculum and the introduction of the CS4All initiative.

Exploring how CS course offerings changed over time and which schools offered CS classes allows us to better understand student enrollment patterns. Implications and solutions to any disparities in enrollment critically depend on the extent to which differences are related to disparities in access vs. differential take up; meaning, differences in enrollment rates even when a student attends a school that offers CS. It is worth noting that our data sample ends with 2018, but that CPS reports that all district-run high schools are offering CS as of the fall of 2019.[37]

Study Sample

We study CS course offerings and student enrollment and performance from fall 2008 through spring 2018. We rely on students' course schedule information to determine both whether a school offered at least one CS course and whether a student enrolled and earned credits in any CS course. Because grade files were not available to us for students attending charter high schools,[38] and course requirements are different for students attending non-traditional schools, such as Options Schools and special education schools, we are missing information for the roughly 30 percent of high school students who were enrolled in charter or non-traditional high schools. As such, we limited the analysis to the 311,314 students enrolled in 108 CPS high schools during the time period studied (**see Appendix A** for more detailed information on the study sample and student demographics). We use this *annual sample* to analyze trends over time in schools offering CS and student enrollment and grades in CS classes. Although this

---

37 See CPS Office of Computer Science website, "Where Can My Child Take Computer Science" https://sites.google.com/cps. edu/cs4all/for-parents/where-can-my-child-take-cs

38 Many CPS charter schools use different student data systems. Creating linkages across these systems is difficult, and our data archive currently does not include records of charter school students' course performance.

approach tells us what was happening each school year, it does not tell us whether a higher share of students took CS at some point in high school or whether more students took multiple courses while others still took none.

Therefore, in order to take a closer look into the experiences of high school students over their first four years of high school, we also examine seven ninth-grade cohorts attending CPS high schools (*the cohort sample*). This cohort sample included students who were first-time ninth-graders in the school years 2008–09, 2009–10, 2010–11, 2011–12, 2012–13, 2013–14, and 2014–15.[39] For comparison, we also included three more recent cohorts (2015–16, 2016–17, 2017–18) for some analyses, but these cohorts had been enrolled in high school fewer than four years by the end of our data sample, spring 2018. In addition, only students in cohorts 2016–17 and 2017–18 were subject to the new CS graduation requirement.[40]

In the cohort sample, we keep any student who was enrolled in any CPS high school in ninth grade, as long as they were enrolled in one of the 108 high schools in our sample for at least one of their first four years of high school. This means that we exclude any student who transferred into CPS from outside the district after ninth grade. Some students in the cohort sample will be missing course-taking data for some school years because they enrolled in a charter or non-traditional high school at some point during their first four years of high school,[41] they dropped out of high school, or they did not enroll for one year of their first four years of high school.

CS Offerings: Changes Over Time

The share of CPS high schools offering at least one CS course more than doubled since 2009. **Figure 2** displays the percentage and number of CPS high schools offering at least one CS course from school year 2008–09 to 2017–18. We considered a school to be offering a CS course if at least five students were enrolled in a CS course. In 2009, only 32 high schools (34 percent) offered at least one CS course, while by 2018, 72 schools (80 percent) offered at least one CS course. Most of this increase occurred following the launch of the CS4All initiative in December 2013.

This increase in the number of high schools offering a CS course led to an increase in the share of students with access to at least one CS course in their high school. Given that larger schools—those with a larger student body—were more likely to offer CS (**see Table 1**), the proportion of students that had access to CS courses increased considerably more than is suggested by the proportion of schools. In 2009, 52 percent of students in CPS high schools were enrolled in one of the 32 high schools offering at least one CS course. By 2018, 92 percent of students enrolled in a CPS high school that offered at least one CS course. Despite the expansion of CS offerings in CPS during our study period, 20 percent of high schools still did not offer any CS course in 2018. Further expanding CS access to the remaining 8 percent of students enrolled in these schools may have been challenging, as they may have faced more difficult obstacles that prevented them from accomplishing this goal sooner.

With the introduction of the ECS curriculum in 2012–13, we can distinguish between introductory level courses (primarily the ECS course), intermediate-level CS courses, and AP CS courses. The intro-level ECS course provides an overview of different CS topics; while intermediate-level courses offer a more in-depth study of specific CS areas, such as robotics, IT problem solving, human-computer interactions, and programming. The shaded areas in **Figure 2** break out the percentages of high schools offering different types of CS courses for 2013 through 2018. Relative to 2013, there has been an expansion in the share of schools

---

39 Most students graduate within four years of attending high school. In the seven cohorts studied, between 75 and 84 percent of students graduated in four years. If we consider graduation within five years instead, graduation rates increase by 4–5 percentage points for the earlier cohorts and only 1 percentage point for the most recent cohort studied.

40 Not all cohorts were used for each analysis. For example, since students in most recent cohorts have not yet completed four years in high school, we used the cohort 2014–15 as the most recent cohort with complete data. However, in some cases we do include these more recent cohorts, as some of these students are subject to the new CS graduation requirement and their outcomes will be relevant to policymakers and practitioners. See Appendix A Table A.4 for a description on which cohorts were used for each analysis.

41 In our cohort sample, about 16 percent of students (cohorts 2008–09 to 2014–15) had less than four years of course-taking data, due to being enrolled in a charter or non-traditional school at some point during their first four years in high school.

The Percentage of CPS Schools Offering CS Courses Increased Over Time, Particularly Since CS4All

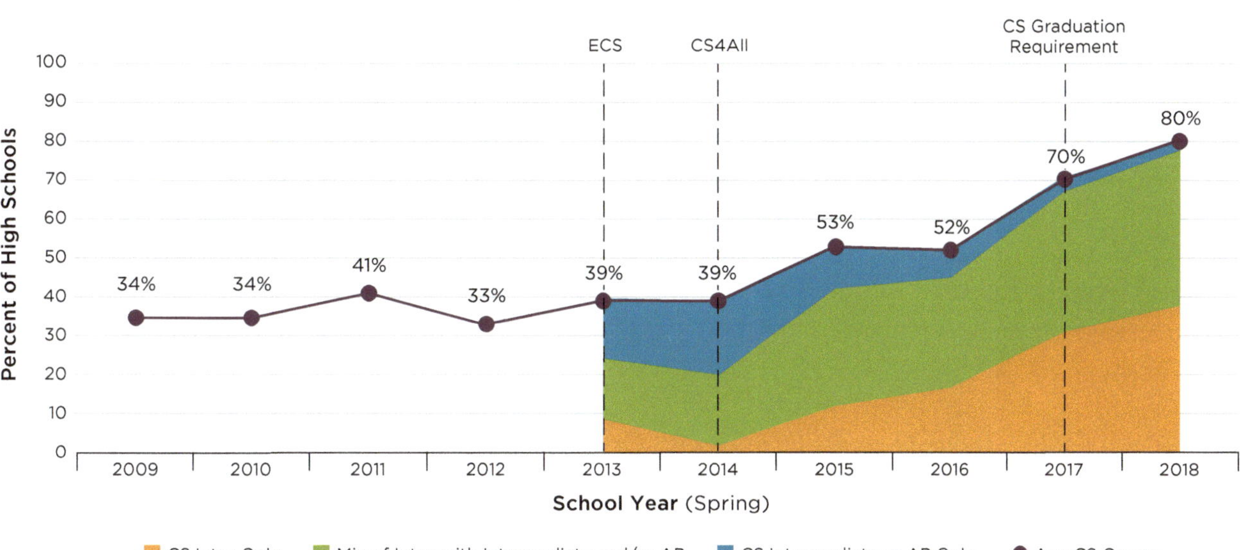

Note: Labels indicate the percentage of high schools in which at least five students were enrolled in any CS course. The higher percentage of schools offering CS course(s) in school year 2010–11 relative to surrounding years may be due to a course code redefinition within CTE programs that took place around the same time. Prior to 2013 there was inconsistency among CS course titles and numbers, which made it difficult to determine which specific levels of CS courses were offered.

offering introductory-level or a mix of introductory- and intermediate-level CS courses. In 2018, 38 percent of high schools offered only an introductory CS course, 2 percent offered only AP and/or intermediate-level CS courses, and 40 percent offered a mix of introductory and AP/intermediate-level CS courses. Thus by 2018, 78 percent of high schools were offering at least one introductory-level course, whether in combination with other CS courses or as a standalone option. This is up from 24 percent of schools offering at least one introductory-level course in 2013, when 8 percent offered only an introductory-level course, 15 percent offered only an AP/intermediate-level CS course, and 16 percent offered a mix of CS course levels.

The increase in CS offerings over recent years has primarily been driven by the expansion of the ECS curriculum in CPS. However, there has also been an increase in the share of CPS high schools offering AP CS courses; only 6 percent of high schools offered AP CS in 2013, compared with 18 percent in 2018. Schools offering a mix of course-levels enable students with no CS exposure to take an introductory-level course as well as go on to take a more advanced CS course. Schools offering only introductory-level courses limit students' ability to continue in CS, and schools offering only more advanced-level courses limit the ability of students without CS exposure outside of high school to get a broader foundational knowledge about CS.

In order to consider the geographic distribution of CPS high schools which offered CS courses, we aggregated Chicago community areas into the nine geographic regions used by the city for planning purposes.[42] During the 2011–12 school year, just prior to the introduction of the ECS curriculum, high schools located in the northern side of the city were the most likely to offer at least one CS course. High schools located on the northern side of the city were generally the most likely to offer at least one CS course. Fifty percent of high schools located in the Northwest Side offered CS in 2012, followed by 40 percent of schools in the Far North Side and North Side

---

42 Each geographic region or "side" is made up of several Chicago community areas. See Appendix A for information about the community areas that were included in each region.

(see Figure 3). Next, 44 percent of high schools located in the Far South Side were offering CS. In the rest of the city, less than one-third of high schools in each region were offering any CS class in that year. For example, in the Central region, neither of the two CPS high schools active in 2012 were offering a CS course.

Following both the introduction of ECS and the CS4All initiative, the number of CPS high schools offering at least one CS course expanded in each geographic region. In 2018, we can see that many high schools not offering CS courses in the 2011–12 school year were offering at least one CS course by spring 2018. For example, all of the high schools located in the Central and Far Southwest Side regions offered CS in spring 2018. In all other regions, more than 60 percent of high schools offered at least one CS course in spring 2018.

High schools located in one of the north side regions of the city—Northwest Side, Far North Side, and North Side—remained more likely (83–90 percent) to offer CS in 2017–18 than other regions of the city. Only 64 percent of high schools located in the South Side region offered any CS course by spring 2018, although this was double the share that were offering CS in 2011–12 (31 percent).

CS Offerings by School Characteristics

Although access to CS increased in Chicago during our study period, 20 percent of high schools were not offering any kind of CS course in spring 2018. **Table 1** presents the share of high schools that were offering at least one CS course by school characteristic. For this exercise, we break down the percentage of CPS high schools offering at least one CS course by school type and size in both 2012 and 2018, before and after the implementation of ECS and CS4All. Table 1 also includes the overall number of high schools in each category and school year.

School Type

High schools were categorized into three types: 1) neighborhood high schools (those which have specific attendance-area boundaries), 2) selective enrollment high schools, and 3) other citywide high schools (those without an attendance-area boundary that also do not offer any selective enrollment program, such as military academies and magnet schools).

Among the three types of high schools, selective enrollment high schools were the most likely to offer

Increases in CS Course Access Were Geographically Widespread

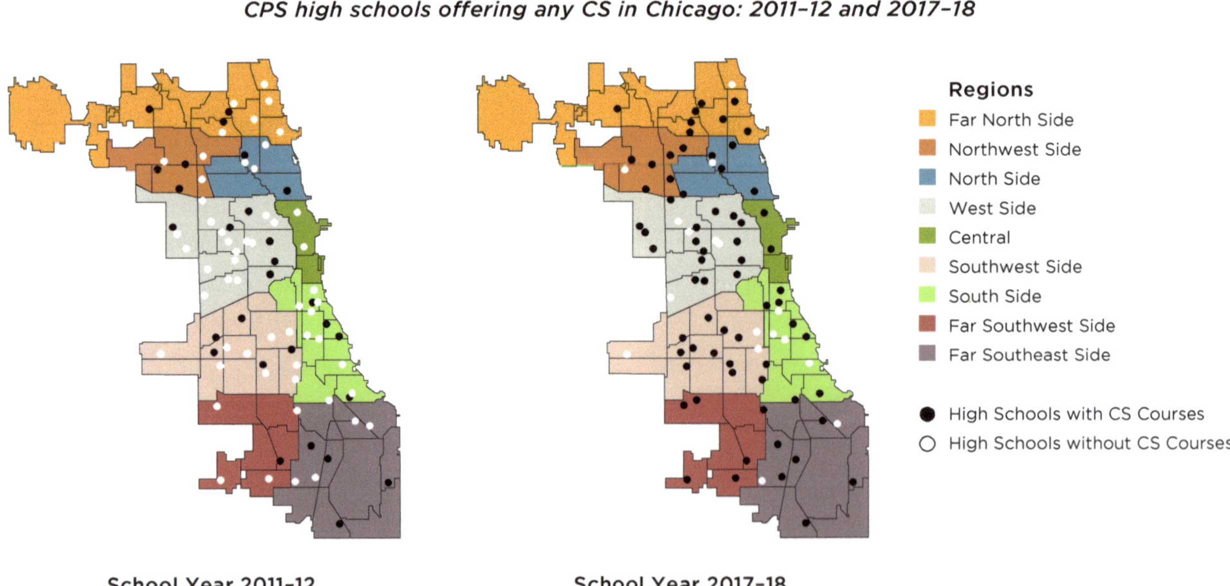

Note: Dots represent the geographical locations of each CPS high school in Chicago in 2012 (left) and 2018 (right); charter and non-traditional high schools are not included. The total number of schools in each geographical area may differ across years due to some schools closing and new schools opening. For more detail regarding these areas, see Appendix A.

	SY 2011–12		SY 2017–18	
	Number of High Schools in Each Category	**Percent Offering Any CS Course**	**Number of High Schools in Each Category**	**Percent Offering Any CS Course**
School Type				
Neighborhood	54	31%	49	76%
Other Citywide	29	24%	30	80%
Selective Enrollment	9	67%	11	100%
Total School Enrollment				
Fewer than 500 Students	29	14%	38	68%
500–899 Students	27	19%	19	79%
900+ Students	36	58%	33	94%

Note: Table does not include charter and non-traditional CPS high schools; see *Study Sample* on p.11 for more details.

at least one CS course in any school year. The number of selective enrollment high schools increased over time, but in 2018 all were offering CS. Although access to CS courses was lower in the other types of high schools, the shares of neighborhood and other citywide high schools offering at least one CS course more than doubled between spring 2012 and spring 2018 to 76 and 80 percent, respectively.

School Size

School size is defined based on overall student enrollment. For this analysis, we divided high schools into three categories: 1) schools with fewer than 500 students, 2) schools with student enrollment between 500 and 899, and 3) schools enrolling 900 or more students.

Larger high schools, those with 900 or more students enrolled, were more likely than smaller high schools to offer CS courses. In 2012, 58 percent of the largest high schools were offering CS, compared with 14 and 19 percent of smaller schools serving less than 500 students and between 500 and 899 students, respectively.

Although access to CS increased for students enrolled in both small and large high schools, only 68 percent of the smallest high schools (less than 500 students enrolled) in spring 2018 offered any computer science course compared to 94 percent of largest high schools (900 or more students).

Summary

CS offerings in CPS increased steadily following the announcement of the CS4All initiative. This expansion ensured that, by spring 2018, 80 percent of high schools offered at least one CS course. But one-fifth of high schools were not offering any type of CS course in spring 2018, despite some currently-enrolled students being subject to the graduation requirement. Overall, we find that these were mostly small high schools. As a result, 92 percent of students in spring 2018 were enrolled in a high school that offered at least one CS course. CPS reports that in the 2019–20 school year, all district-run high schools offered CS. This is good news, given that the majority of students graduating in spring 2020 need to meet the new CS graduation requirement. Going forward, high schools will need to continue to offer enough CS classes to serve roughly one-quarter of their total enrollment in each school year, in order for all students to meet the graduation requirement.

CHAPTER 2

Enrollment in Computer Science

Key Takeaways on CS Enrollment

- **Annual enrollment in CS courses increased** steadily since the introduction of ECS, mostly driven by enrollment in introductory-level courses.

- **Cohort enrollment rates increased over time.** Only 8 percent of the 2010–11 cohort took at least one CS course after four years of high school, compared with 26 percent of the 2014–15 cohort.
  - The increase in enrollment rates across cohorts was largely driven by an increase in ninth-grade enrollment rates.
  - Ninth-grade enrollment rates increased even more sharply for the first two cohorts that were subject to the new CS graduation requirement, exceeding in only one year the enrollment rates for prior cohorts after four years of high school.

- **Differences in enrollment rates by race/ethnicity and neighborhood SES** were related to differences in access to CS.
  - While Black students were the least likely to enroll in a CS course, these students were also the least likely to attend a school that offered CS. Once we account for differences in access to CS, Black students were the most likely to enroll in a CS course. Asian students were also more likely than average to enroll in a CS course, even after adjusting for access, while Latino and White students were somewhat less likely than average to enroll in a CS course.

  - Students living in the lowest-SES neighborhoods were 3 percentage points less likely to enroll in a CS course, relative to the overall average; however, differences in access to a CS course also drove this enrollment difference. Once we account for access to a CS course, students living in the lowest-SES neighborhoods were about as likely as the average student to enroll in a CS course.

  - Male students were more likely to enroll in a CS course than female students. Because female students were somewhat more likely to attend a school that offered CS, this difference widens when we account for access to CS.

- **For the 2014–15 cohort, the characteristics of students enrolled in introductory-level CS courses** more closely reflected the CPS high school population than the characteristics of students enrolled in intermediate-level or AP CS courses. This was also true relative to introductory-level CS students in the 2010–11 cohort.

In Chapter 1, we described the expansion in the number of CPS high schools offering CS courses. We now switch the focus to describe how student enrollment in CS courses evolved with the steady expansion of CS offerings over the past decade. We also examine changes in CS enrollment rates by grade-level, gender, race/ethnicity, and neighborhood SES. For these analyses, CS enrollment is defined as taking any type of CS class, regardless of its level. However, we also compare student enrollment in introductory and more advanced (intermediate and AP) courses. It is important to keep in mind that during most of the school years analyzed in this report, CS classes were elective courses. Thus, students who enrolled in a CS course may have had interests and characteristics that differed from students who did not elect to take a CS course. Although CS was no longer an elective for students in the 2016–17 and 2017–18 cohorts, there may still have been differences in interests and characteristics between students who took a CS course in ninth or tenth grade, compared with students who waited to take a CS course in eleventh or twelfth grade.

We begin by using the annual sample to look at the share of all high school students enrolled in a CS course in each school year from 2008–09 to 2017–18. This tells us whether more students took CS each year, but it does not tell us whether more students were taking CS at some point in high school. This increase in course-taking could reflect that some students were taking multiple courses while others still took none. Therefore, using the cohort sample, we also look at enrollment in CS over the course of students' time in high school, following cohorts of students from their ninth-grade year through their twelfth-grade year.

For the cohort sample, we defined seven cohorts of students based on their first-time ninth-grade school year (2008–09, 2009–10, 2010–11, 2011–12, 2012–13, 2013–14, and 2014–15). We follow these cohorts through their first four years in high school, looking at both their cumulative enrollment rates through each year of high school as well as their cohort enrollment rates at the end of high school (i.e., their cumulative enrollment rates at the end of their first four years of high school). For comparison, we also include three recent cohorts (2015–16, 2016–17, and 2017–18); these cohorts were enrolled in high school for fewer than four years as of spring 2018. One challenge in using cohorts is that students may transfer from, or into, CPS charter or non-traditional schools during their high school years, but we do not have course-taking information data from these schools. To address this, we include all students who were enrolled in a high school in our sample during at least one of their first four years in high school, with one exception: we exclude students who transfer into CPS from outside the district after ninth grade.[43]

Student Enrollment in CS: Changes Over Time

Prior to the introduction of the ECS curriculum, between 2 and 3 percent of all high school students each year were taking at least one CS course. By 2018, that share increased to 20 percent.

As introductory CS courses became available in more CPS high schools, student enrollment in this type of course increased at a faster rate than enrollment in more advanced CS courses (intermediate or AP CS). From spring 2013 to spring 2018, the share of students in each year enrolled in an introductory CS course increased by 12 percentage points; in contrast, the share of students enrolled in only more advanced CS courses increased by only 2 percentage points over the same period. In 2018, 73 percent of the students enrolled in a CS class were taking an introductory-level course, up from around 50 percent in 2013 (**see Figure 4**).

In order to understand changes over time in the share of students who took at least one CS course, we rely on the *cohort sample* for the analyses presented in the rest of the chapter. For each cohort (defined by the school year of first-time, ninth-grade enrollment), **Figure 5** shows the cumulative percentage of students who took at least one CS course by the end of four years of high school. If every student in a cohort took at least one CS course, the twelfth-grade percentage would equal 100. For the earliest cohorts (2008–09, 2009–10, and 2010–11), student participation in CS showed little change across cohorts, and therefore the cumulative enrollment lines are virtually identical. Less than 2 percent of students in the earliest three cohorts enrolled in at least one CS course by the end of their ninth-grade year, and less than 10 percent had enrolled in at least one CS course by the end of their twelfth-grade year. However, since the 2010–11 cohort, enrollment rates in CS have been increasing; 6 percent of the 2012–13 cohort and 12 percent of the 2014–15 cohort enrolled in at least one CS course by the end of their ninth-grade year, and 18 and 25 percent of these cohorts, respectively, enrolled in at least one CS course by the end of their first four years of high school. These increases in enrollment rates by the end of four years of high school were largely driven by increases in ninth-grade enrollment, as evidenced by the nearly parallel upward shift of the cumulative enrollment rates. In other words, the share of students taking their first CS course in ninth grade increased across cohorts, but the shares of students taking their first CS course in grades 10–12 stayed relatively constant.

We see a sharp increase in CS enrollment for the first two cohorts subject to the CS graduation requirement (2016–17 and 2017–18). By the end of their ninth-grade year, 28 percent of students in the 2016–17 cohort and

---

Annual Enrollment in CS Courses Increased Steadily Post-ECS

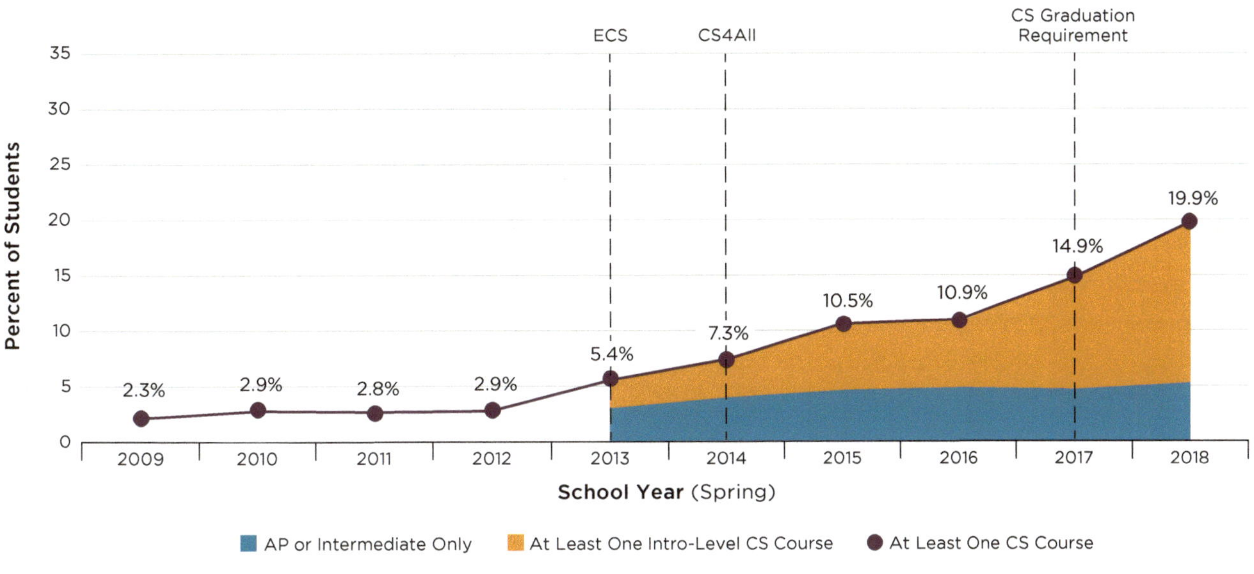

Note: The percent of students taking at least one introductory-level CS course includes both students who only took an introductory course and students who took both an introductory-level and more advanced (intermediate or AP) level course. Less than 1 percent of all students are in this latter category.

Cohort Enrollment Rates Increased Over Time, Especially for Those Subject to the CS Graduation Requirement

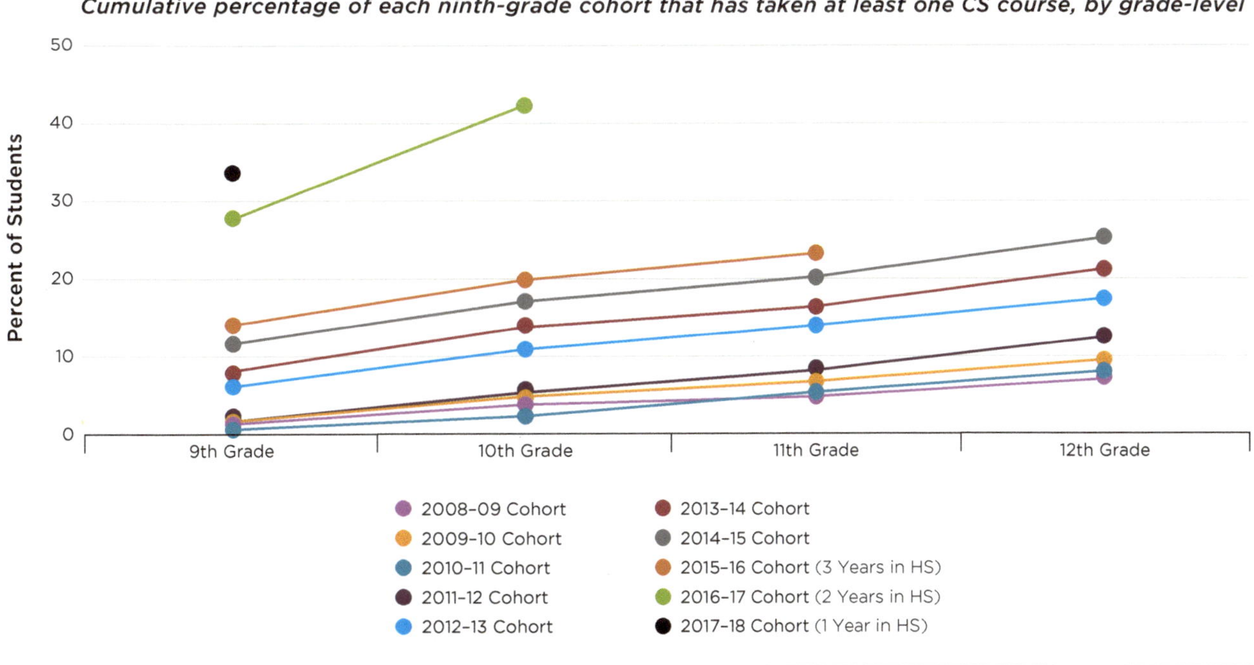

Note: Each series corresponds to a ninth-grade cohort, labeled by the ninth-grade school year. Data for this study are only available through the 2017–18 school year, so cumulative enrollment rates are missing for later grades of the most recent three cohorts. Both the 2016–17 and 2017–18 cohorts were subject to the CPS graduation requirement of earning at least one credit in CS.

34 percent of students in the 2017–18 cohort enrolled in at least one CS course. These enrollment rates, after only one year of high school, exceeded prior cohorts' cumulative enrollment rates after four years of high school. While 28 percent of students in the 2016–17 cohort took their first CS courses in ninth grade, only an additional 14 percent of the cohort took their first CS course in tenth grade. If a similar 14 percent of the cohort takes their first CS course in each of eleventh and twelfth grade, only 71 percent of the 2016–17 cohort will have taken at least one CS course by the end of their first four years in high school.[44] Thus, the CS graduation requirement could delay graduation for some students in the 2016–17 cohort if enrollment rates do not pick up in eleventh and twelfth grade. That said, select students are able to waive the CS graduation requirement.[45] These waivers may help explain why cumulative rates remained below 50 percent for the 2016–17 cohort at the end of tenth grade.

CS Enrollment Differences by Student Characteristics

Gender Differences

Across cohorts, male students were more likely than female students to enroll in any type of CS course (**see Figure 6**). The ECS curriculum was designed to be culturally relevant and broaden participation in CS. After its introduction in 2013, cohort enrollment rates increased for both male and female students, but the increase was faster for male students. Male students were more likely than their female peers to take advantage of this new CS opportunity. For the 2010–11 cohort, the difference in CS enrollment rates between male and female students over the first four years of high school was about 4 percentage points. The enrollment rate difference widened to 9 percentage points for the 2014–15 cohort. We expect this difference to disappear for the cohorts of students subject to the graduation

Male Students Were More Likely Than Female Students to Enroll in a CS Course

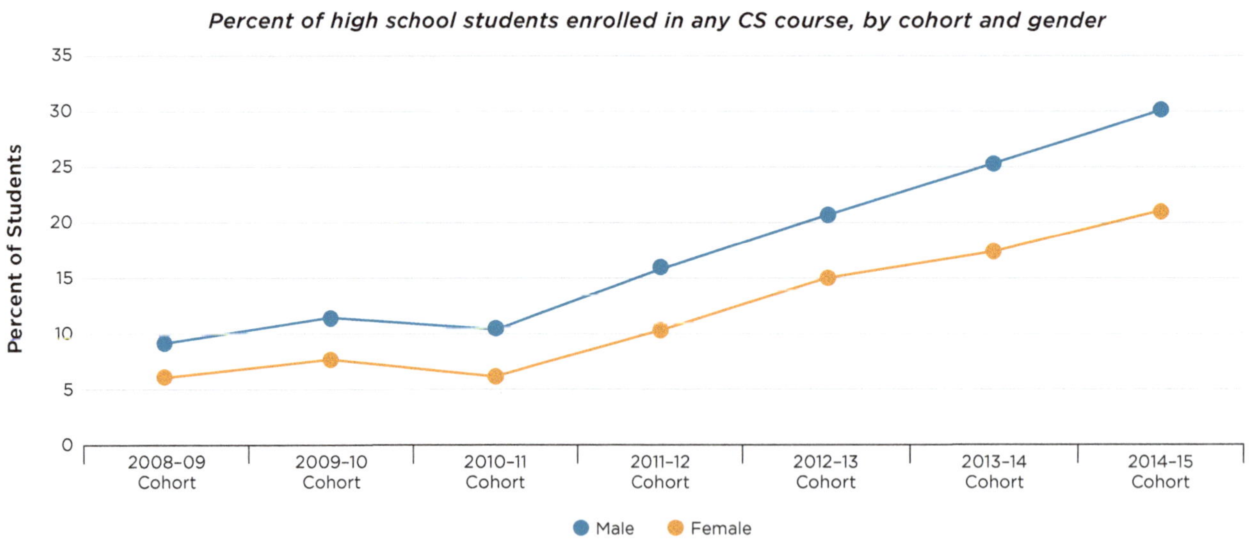

Note: Each series corresponds to a ninth-grade cohort, labeled by the ninth-grade school year.

44 Although the graduation requirement requires students to earn at least one CS credit, which corresponds to two semester CS courses, we show in the next chapter that most students who took at least one CS course had earned at least one credit.
45 See *Computer Science in CPS* on p.7.

requirement. However, if male and female students waive the CS requirement at different rates, gender differences in CS enrollment rates could remain.

Race/Ethnicity Differences

As shown in **Figure 7**, cohort enrollment rates by student race/ethnicity were relatively unchanged between the 2008–09 and 2010–11 cohorts, after which enrollment rates increased for all groups. Across all cohorts, Asian students were the most likely to have taken at least one CS course, and the cohort enrollment rates for Asian students were 7 to 12 percentage points higher than for either Latino or Black students. In contrast, Latino and Black CS enrollment rates increased faster than the White CS enrollment rates, such that the differences in cohort enrollment rates between White students and Latino and Black students narrowed to less than 2 percentage points for the 2014–15 cohort. For the 2014–15 cohort (the most recent cohort in our study with four years' worth of data), cohort enrollment rates were 25 percent for Latino students, 24 percent for Black students, 26 percent for White students, and 34 percent for Asian students.

Socioeconomic Differences

For the first three cohorts in our study, cohort enrollment rates ranged from 5–8 percent for students living in the lowest-SES neighborhoods, to 9–10 percent for students living in the highest-SES neighborhoods (**see Figure 8**).[46] Subsequent cohort enrollment rates rose for all SES groups. However, the rate of increase in cohort enrollment rates for students living in the lowest-SES neighborhoods was slightly slower than for other groups, leading to small increases in the differences between students living in the lowest-SES neighborhoods and all higher-SES groups. For the 2014–15 cohort, 22 percent of students living in the lowest-SES neighborhoods enrolled in at least one CS course, compared with

Asian Students Were Most Likely to Enroll in CS courses, and Enrollment Differences Narrowed Among Black, Latino, and White Students

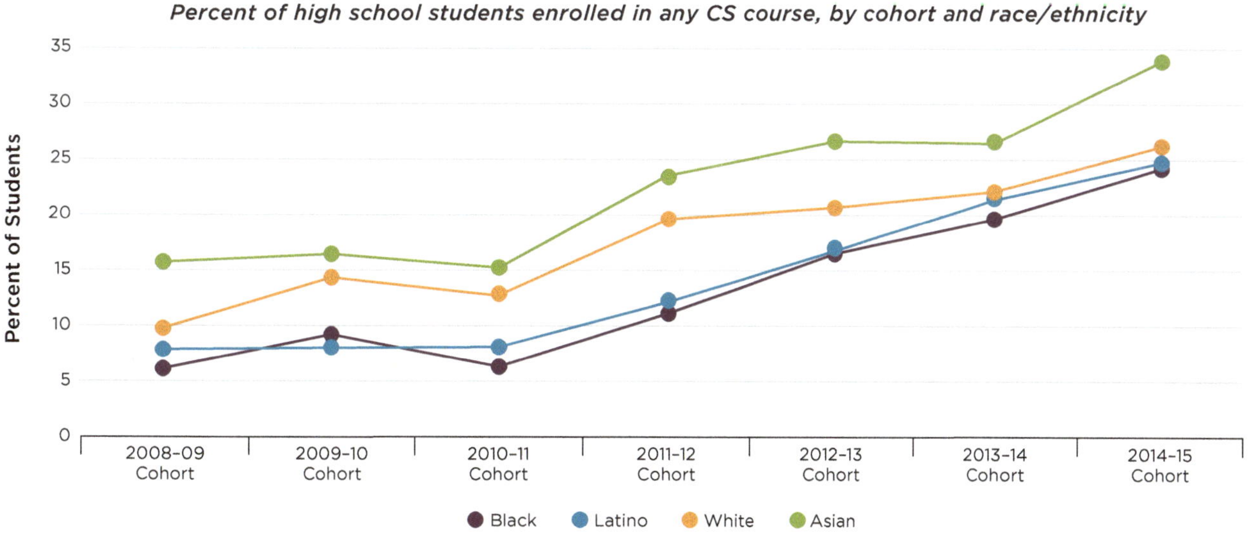

Note: Each series corresponds to a ninth-grade cohort, labeled by the ninth-grade school year. Students from other races/ethnicities, including Native American students and students who listed multiple races/ethnicities, represented 2 percent or less of each cohort, and were not included in the analyses.

46 We measure student SES using a poverty concentration index that measures the percentage of families with income below the poverty line and the percentage of adult males unemployed at the census block group level. We define SES quartiles within year, using 9th-grade students, and assign each student to the SES quartile corresponding to their residential census block group. For students who were not in our sample during ninth grade, we assign the SES quartile based on the first year we observe them in the data.

Students Living in the Lowest-SES Neighborhoods Were Least Likely to Enroll in CS Courses

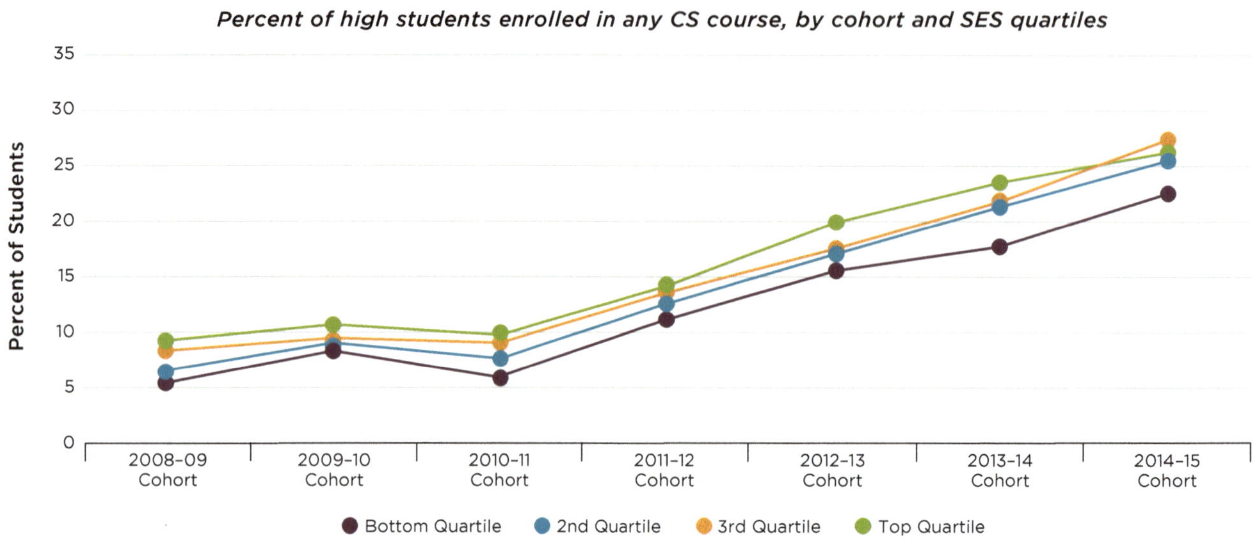

Note: Each series corresponds to a ninth-grade cohort labeled by the ninth-grade school year. Students in the bottom quartile lived in neighborhoods with the greatest poverty concentration (lowest SES).

Student Demographics By CS Course Type

	Cohort Demographics		Introductory-Level CS		Intermediate-Level CS		AP CS	
	2010–11 Cohort	2014–15 Cohort	2010–11 Cohort	2014–15 Cohort	2010–11 Cohort	2014–15 Cohort	2010–11 Cohort	2014–15 Cohort
% Female	50.7	51.3	39.7	43.0	37.0	34.6	22.6	31.2
% Asian	4.4	4.8	5.5	4.3	7.2	7.4	16.7	19.1
% Black	39.9	34.5	25.1	38.9	34.3	35.2	11.8	10.7
% Latino	44.9	48.2	58.3	48.2	43.3	40.3	47.3	42.7
% White	9.3	10.9	9.6	7.1	13.0	15.1	22.0	24.5
% Bottom SES Quartile*	24.4	25.1	20.6	25.5	22.7	23.0	8.1	11.1
Std. 8th Grade Math Test Score**	0.13	0.15	0.08	-0.04	0.35	0.40	1.48	1.14

Note: Cohorts refer to ninth-grade cohort, labeled by the ninth-grade school year. These CS course type demographics are not mutually exclusive, as a student may have taken both an introductory level and a more advanced-level CS course during their four years in high school. *Students living in a neighborhood in the bottom SES quartile, based on the neighborhood concentration of poverty index. **In order to compare across cohorts and tests, students' eighth-grade math test scores (ISAT or NWEA, depending on the cohort) were standardized to have a mean of 0 and a standard deviation of 1; see Appendix A for more detail about test score standardization.

26 to 28 percent of students living in higher-SES neighborhoods (the second through fourth quartiles).

Table 2 illustrates the characteristics of students overall and those who enrolled in CS courses by cohort and CS course level. The first two columns present overall mean characteristics for the 2010–11 and 2014–15 cohorts, respectively. The remaining columns present average characteristics for students who enrolled in at least one CS course, by course type (introductory-level, intermediate-level, or AP). Each column within course type represents a different cohort of students (2010–11 or 2014–15). Within each column, cells represent average characteristics for students who took at least one CS course of that type over their first four years of high school. For example, of all of the students in the 2010–11 cohort who took at least one introductory-level class during their first four years in high school, 39.7 percent were female.

While the share of students enrolled in an introductory-level or AP CS course who were female increased between the 2010–11 and 2014–15 cohorts, a higher share of students were male at all CS course levels. Further, the male-female enrollment difference was larger in more advanced CS courses than the male-female enrollment difference in introductory-level courses.

By race/ethnicity group, students in the 2014–15 cohort who enrolled in introductory-level courses were roughly representative of the cohort as a whole (**see Table A.3 in Appendix A** for overall cohort characteristics). Forty-eight percent of students enrolled in an introductory-level course were Latino, 39 percent were Black, 7 percent were White, and 4 percent were Asian. In comparison, the overall cohort population was 48 percent Latino, 35 percent Black, 11 percent White, and 5 percent Asian. In intermediate-level and AP courses, a disproportionate share of students enrolled were White or Asian. This was true for both the 2010–11 and 2014–15 cohorts. In fact, the over-representation of White and Asian students enrolled in AP CS courses increased between the 2010–11 and 2014–15 cohorts.

Representation of students from the lowest-SES neighborhoods improved for all class types between the 2010–11 and 2014–15 cohorts. For the 2014–15 cohort, 25 percent of students enrolled in at least one introductory-level CS course during the first four years of high school were living in a neighborhood in the bottom quartile of neighborhood SES, up from 21 percent of introductory-level CS course students in the 2010–11 cohort. However, the share of students enrolled in AP CS courses who lived in the lowest-SES neighborhoods remained below 15 percent.

Finally, students who enrolled in more advanced CS courses had, on average, higher prior math achievement than students who took an introductory-level CS course. Namely, students enrolled in introductory-level CS scored about average in terms of standardized eighth-grade math test scores, while students who took at least one intermediate-level CS course scored about 0.4 standard deviations above the average, and students who enrolled in AP CS scored more than one standard deviation above average.

Enrollment Differences and Access to CS

Differences in enrollment rates by race/ethnicity and neighborhood SES were related to differences in access to CS, as Black, Latino, and students living in high-poverty neighborhoods were less likely to attend a school offering CS. As shown in preceding sections, students' likelihood of enrolling in a CS course differed by gender, race/ethnicity, and neighborhood SES. For instance, male students and Asian students were more likely to enroll in a CS course than female students or students of other race/ethnicity groups, respectively. However, student body characteristics differed across high schools, so differences in CS course availability across high schools may have contributed to differences in CS enrollment, especially by student race/ethnicity and neighborhood SES. For example, if high schools with larger populations of Black students were less likely to offer CS, this lack of access may help us understand why Black students were less likely to have enrolled in a CS course when looking at district-wide CS enrollment rates.

We limit the sample to students in the 2014–15 cohort who were enrolled in a high school that offered at least one CS course over their first four years of high school. We then use regression analysis in order to assess the importance of access in contributing to enrollment differences in CS courses by gender, race/ethnicity, and neighborhood SES. Specifically, we consider how enrolling in at least one CS course during the first four years of high school relates to student demographic characteristics such as gender, race/ethnicity, and neighborhood SES, while also including an indicator for the number of years—one to four—that a student was enrolled in a high school that offered at least one CS course (**see Table B.1. in Appendix B**). Students in the 2014–15 cohort began high school following the adoption of the ECS curriculum and the announcement of the CS4All initiative. As a result, this cohort was more likely than students from prior cohorts to have attended a high school that was offering at least one CS course.[47]

---

47 Using the same analysis, we find similar patterns for the 2008–09 cohort which graduated prior to both the adoption of the ECS curriculum and the CS4All initiative; the gender difference remained even after accounting for CS access, while race/ethnicity differences changed, and SES differences narrowed.

Figures 9 through 11 display the CS enrollment rate differences, relative to the average enrollment rate, by student gender (Figure 9), race/ethnicity (Figure 10), and neighborhood SES (Figure 11). The first set of bars in these figures represents the overall enrollment rate difference between the average student and that particular student group. These reflect the enrollment rates illustrated in Figures 6 through 8, relative to the mean enrollment rate. The second set of bars represents these same enrollment rate differences when we only consider students who were enrolled in a school that offered at least one CS course during a student's first four years of high school. We additionally account for the number of years enrolled in a school offering CS and the other demographic characteristics. By limiting the sample to students who attended a high school offering CS and including indicators for the number of years a student was enrolled in a high school that offered CS, we are able to estimate how much of the remaining differences in enrollment rates were associated with students' gender, race/ethnicity, and neighborhood SES.

Figure 9 displays differences in CS enrollment rates for male and female students, relative to the overall average. The unadjusted differences (first panel) indicate that young men were 4.6 percentage points more likely than average to enroll in a CS course while young women were 4.5 percentage points less likely to enroll in a CS course, meaning there was a roughly 9 percentage point difference in enrollment rates between male and female students.[48] Because female students are somewhat more likely than male students to attend high schools that offered CS, such as selective enrollment high schools, this difference increases once we account for access to CS (second panel). When looking at the probability of enrolling in a CS class conditional on access to a CS course (while also controlling for race/ethnicity and neighborhood SES), female students were less likely than male students to take advantage of the opportunity to enroll in a CS course. Specifically, young men were 6 percentage points more likely than average to enroll in a CS course, and young women were roughly 6 percentage points less likely than average to enroll in a CS

Male Students Were More Likely to Enroll in At Least One CS Course, Even After Accounting for Access to CS

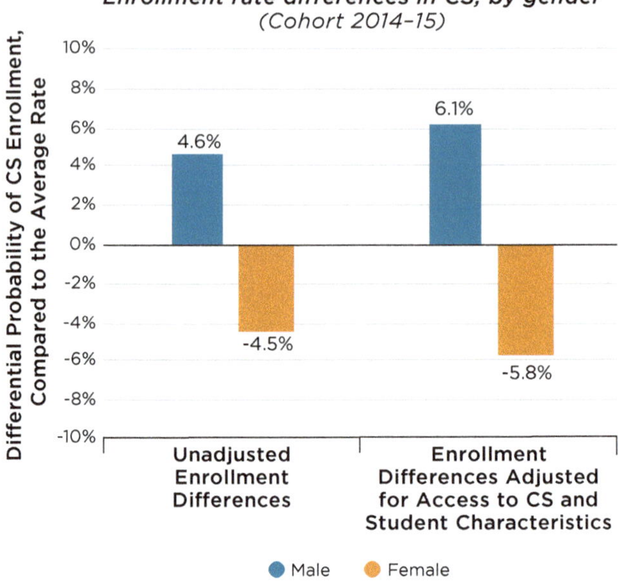

Note: Regression analyses that estimate the adjusted enrollment differences include indicators for years of access to CS, gender, race/ethnicity, and neighborhood SES quartile. The difference between the relative enrollment rates equals the overall (adjusted or unadjusted) enrollment rate difference for students in the 2014–15 ninth-grade cohort. For example, the difference in adjusted enrollment rates between male and female students is roughly 12 percentage points.

course for a roughly 12 percentage point enrollment rate difference between male and female students.

Figure 10 presents differences in the probability of enrolling in at least one CS course by student race/ethnicity relative to the average enrollment rate. The unadjusted differences (first panel) indicate that Asian students' enrollment rate in CS courses was 8 percentage points higher than the overall average enrollment rate for the 2014–15 cohort. Enrollment rates for all other race/ethnicity groups included in the analyses—Latino, Black, and White—were within 1 percentage point above or below the cohort average enrollment rate. However, 97 percent of Asian students in the 2014–15 cohort enrolled in a school that offered CS, compared with only 77 percent of Black students. Thus, when we account for access to CS in a regression framework (second panel), Asian students were only 1.5 percentage points more likely than average to enroll in a CS course, while Black students were 4 percentage

---

48 These differences are not equal in absolute value because slightly more than 50 percent of students in our sample are female.

Black Students Were the Most Likely to Enroll in a CS Course, After Accounting for Access to CS

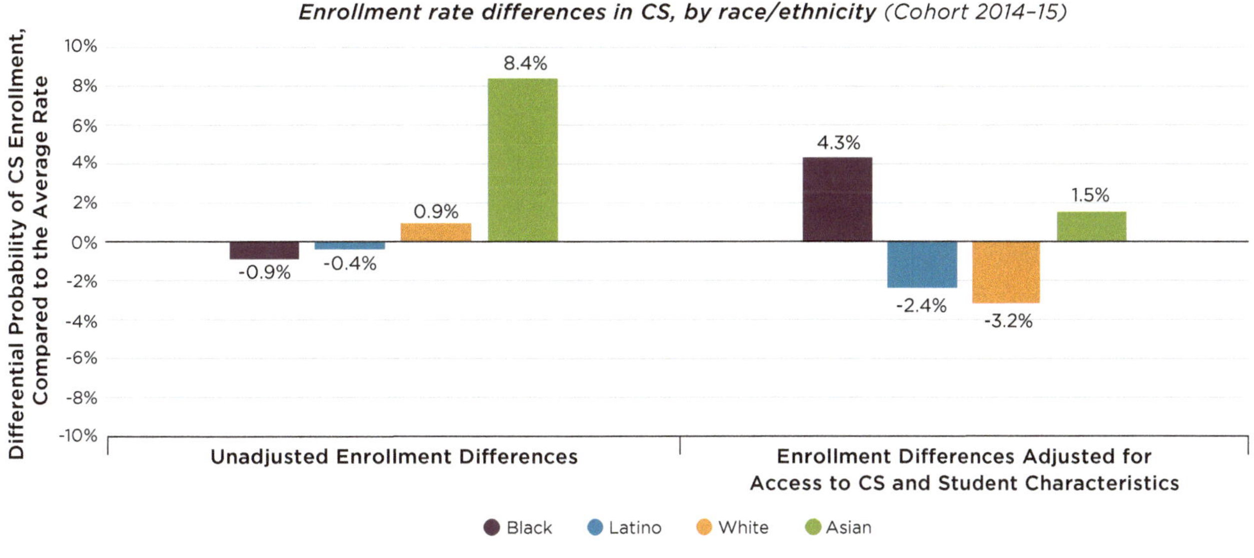

Note: Regression analyses that estimate the adjusted enrollment differences include indicators for years of access to CS, gender, race/ethnicity, and neighborhood SES quartile. The difference between the relative enrollment rates for two groups equals the overall (adjusted or unadjusted) enrollment rate difference between those two groups in the 2014–15 ninth-grade cohort. For example, the difference in adjusted enrollment rates between Black and Latino students is roughly 7 percentage points.

Differences in CS Enrollment Rates by Neighborhood SES Were Small, After Accounting for Access to CS

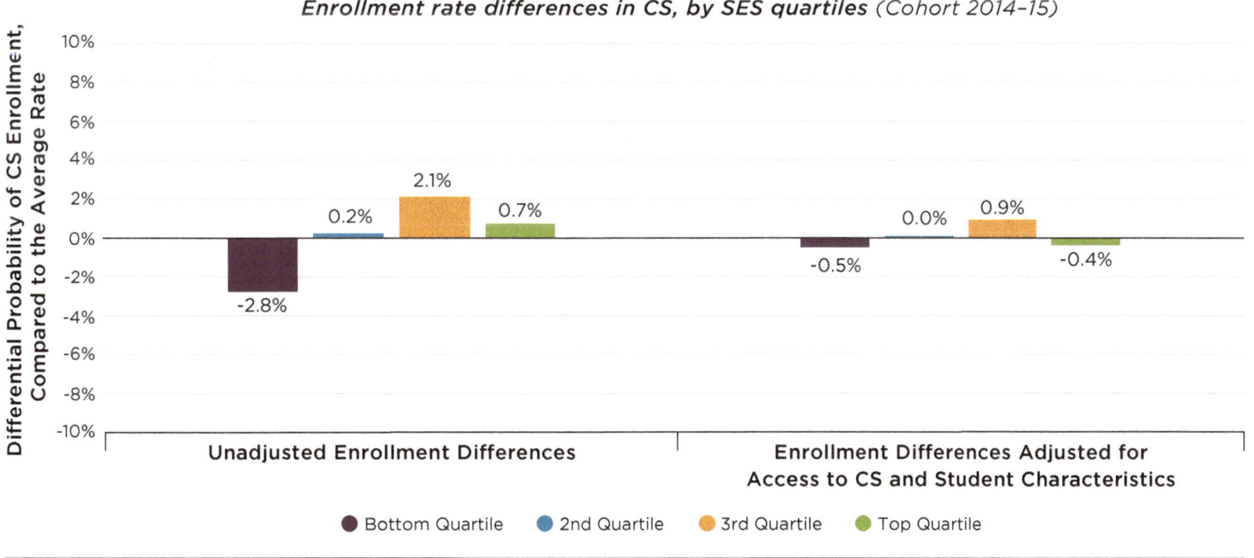

Note: Students in the bottom quartile lived in neighborhoods with the greatest poverty concentration (lowest SES). Regression analyses that estimate the adjusted enrollment differences include indicators for years of access to CS, gender, race/ethnicity, and neighborhood SES quartile. The difference between the relative enrollment rates for two groups equals the overall (adjusted or unadjusted) enrollment rate difference between those two groups for students in the 2014–15 ninth-grade cohort. For example, the difference in adjusted enrollment rates between students from the bottom and top SES quartiles is roughly 0 percentage points.

points more likely than average to enroll in a CS course. Latino students and White students were less likely than average to have enrolled in at least one CS course, reflecting that when Latino and White students had access to CS, they were less likely to take advantage of the opportunity than were Black and Asian students

(see Table B.1 in Appendix B). Large differences in districtwide enrollment rates between Asian students and other race/ethnicity groups arose in part due to differences in access to CS.

Figure 11 presents differences in CS enrollment rates for each of the SES quartiles, relative to the overall average enrollment rate. Students in the bottom quartile lived in the lowest-SES neighborhoods, while students in the top quartile lived in the highest-SES neighborhoods. Enrollment rate differences were smaller across neighborhood SES groups than across student race/ethnicity groups. The unadjusted enrollment rate differences (first panel) indicate that students from the lowest-SES neighborhoods (bottom quartile) were 3 percentage points less likely than average to enroll in at least one CS course. Using a regression framework to account for differences in access (second panel) reduces the enrollment rate difference for students from the lowest-SES neighborhoods to only 0.5 percentage points below average. Enrollment rates for students living in higher-SES neighborhoods (quartiles two to four) were also within 1 percentage point above or below the cohort average.

Summary

Enrollment in CS courses increased following the introduction of the introductory-level ECS curriculum in CPS. Through the 2015–16 cohort, the increases were largely driven by increased enrollment among ninth-grade students. Twenty-five percent of students in the 2014–15 cohort (the most recent cohort for which we had four years of course enrollment data) had taken any type of CS course by the end of four years in high school. The 2016–17 and 2017–18 cohorts were the first students to be subject to the new CPS CS graduation requirement. Ninth-grade enrollment rates for these cohorts increased sharply relative to prior cohorts, exceeding in only one year the four-year enrollment rates for prior cohorts. However, only 42 percent of the 2016–17 cohort had enrolled in at least one CS course by the end of tenth grade, suggesting that, absent a pick-up in enrollment rates in eleventh or twelfth grade, the CS graduation requirement could delay graduation for some students unless all students who weren't enrolling were eligible for waivers.

Over time, enrollment rates for some student groups traditionally underrepresented in CS increased. Lower district-wide CS enrollment rates for Black students and for students from the lowest-SES neighborhoods in part reflected differences in access to CS courses. This suggests that districtwide enrollment rates for these groups would increase with expanded access to CS, even without the graduation requirement. In contrast, expansion in CS access alone did not narrow the differences in enrollment rates between male and female students because female students were already somewhat more likely to attend a high school that offered CS. However, because all students are now subject to the new CS graduation requirement, differences in the shares of students taking at least one CS course should decrease. Thus, the CS graduation requirement may better prepare all students for living and working in the modern era in which technology and the need for computational thinking are widespread.

CHAPTER 3

Performance in Computer Science

Key Takeaways on CS Performance

- **Student grades in CS courses rose over time.** By 2018, almost 70 percent of the grades earned in CS classes were As or Bs, and only 4 percent were failing grades.

- **Twenty-one percent of students** in the 2014–15 cohort who graduated in 2018 earned at least one credit in CS. Higher shares of students in the cohorts subject to the graduation requirement earned at least one CS credit in less than four years of high school.

- **Grades in CS courses were higher than grades in core subject courses**, both overall and for all student groups.

In addition to considering enrollment in CS courses, as we did in Chapter 2, it is important to see the performance in CS courses to understand student engagement in these courses and to see whether students enrolling in these courses are actually earning the credit, especially for the cohorts subject to the graduation requirement. When CS courses were elective courses, we can hypothesize that students who enrolled in them were more interested in and motivated by CS than those who did not. Now that CS is a requirement, it is probably the case that some of the students taking CS will be less motivated and interested than before. If these students earn low grades or even fail their CS classes, we might worry that requirements to take CS will bring down students' GPAs and affect their likelihood of graduating from high school on time.

This chapter describes how students performed in CS courses, compared to other core courses, in terms of grades and credits earned.[49] Using the annual sample, we begin by looking at the distribution of grades students earned in their CS courses over time. Next, using the cohort sample, we look at different cohorts of students and the number of CS credits they earned. This is particularly relevant, as earning at least one credit in CS recently became a graduation requirement. If enrollment rates in CS courses are increasing but students are getting Fs,

graduation rates might be affected, since students will not earn a credit for this course.

Additionally, for students who took at least one CS class, we use regression analysis to compare their average GPA in CS to their average GPA in core subject courses taken during the same school year (i.e., math, English, social studies, and science). This approach allows us to compare a student's grades in CS to their grades in core subjects, while accounting for other factors that may be related to their academic performance in a particular school year. We also explore whether there are differences in CS performance by gender, race/ethnicity, or neighborhood SES and compare those to any differences observed in core subjects.

CS Course Grades

Student performance in CS courses remained high over time, with few students failing their classes. **Figure 12** displays the distribution of grades earned in CS courses for each school year. Grades in CS courses were generally high and increased over time. In 2009, 61 percent of the grades in CS classes were in the A or B range. By 2018, 68 percent of the grades earned in CS classes were As or Bs. Likewise, the percentage of failing grades in any CS course (Fs) decreased over the same period.

---

[49] In this analysis, core courses are defined as English, math, science, and social studies.

More Than One-Half of CS Course Grades Were As or Bs

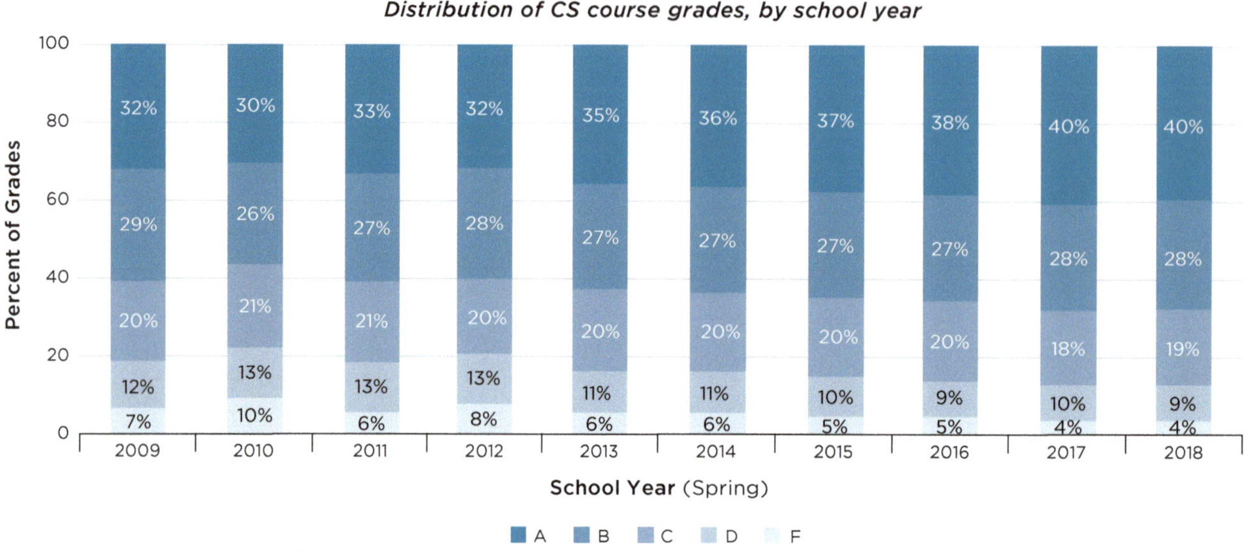

Seven percent of CS grades were Fs in 2009, compared to only 4 percent in 2018. While the share of D grades also diminished (a 3-percentage point decrease from 2009 to 2018), the share of grades in the C category remained relatively constant at about 20 percent, similar to the share of Bs, which remained fairly constant at about 27 percent.

CS Credits Earned

Because few students failed a CS course, increased enrollment in CS courses translated into increases in the share of students earning at least one CS credit. **Figure 13** displays the percentages of students in each cohort earning half a CS credit, one CS credit, and more than one CS credit during their first four years in high school. For comparison, the last three bars represent cohorts that have been enrolled in high school for fewer than four years.

The increase over time in the percentage of students enrolling in at least one CS course led to a similar increase in the percentage of students earning at least one CS credit during four years of high school. For the 2008–09 cohort, only 6 percent of students earned at least one CS credit after four years of high school; this increased to 20 percent for the 2014–15 cohort. The share of students earning more than one credit also increased over time, although this number remains small. Three percent of students in the 2014–15 cohort earned more than one CS credit, up from 1 percent in the 2008–09 cohort.

In the 2014–15 cohort, the last graduating cohort before the introduction of the new graduation requirement, 21 percent of students earned at least one CS credit during their first four years of high school. In contrast, 36 percent of students in the 2016–17 cohort had earned at least one CS credit by the end of only two years of high school, and 28 percent of students in the 2017–18 cohort had earned at least one CS credit by the end of their first year of high school. Students in these two most recent cohorts are subject to the new graduation requirement and must earn at least one CS credit in order to graduate from high school. This requirement likely drove the sharp increase in CS credit accumulation.

CS Course Grades vs. Other Course Grades

To compare CS course grades with other course grades, we focus on students in the ninth-grade cohorts who first enrolled in high school after the introduction

For the 2017–18 Cohort, More Students Earned CS Course Credits in One Year than Many Earlier Cohorts Earned in Four Years

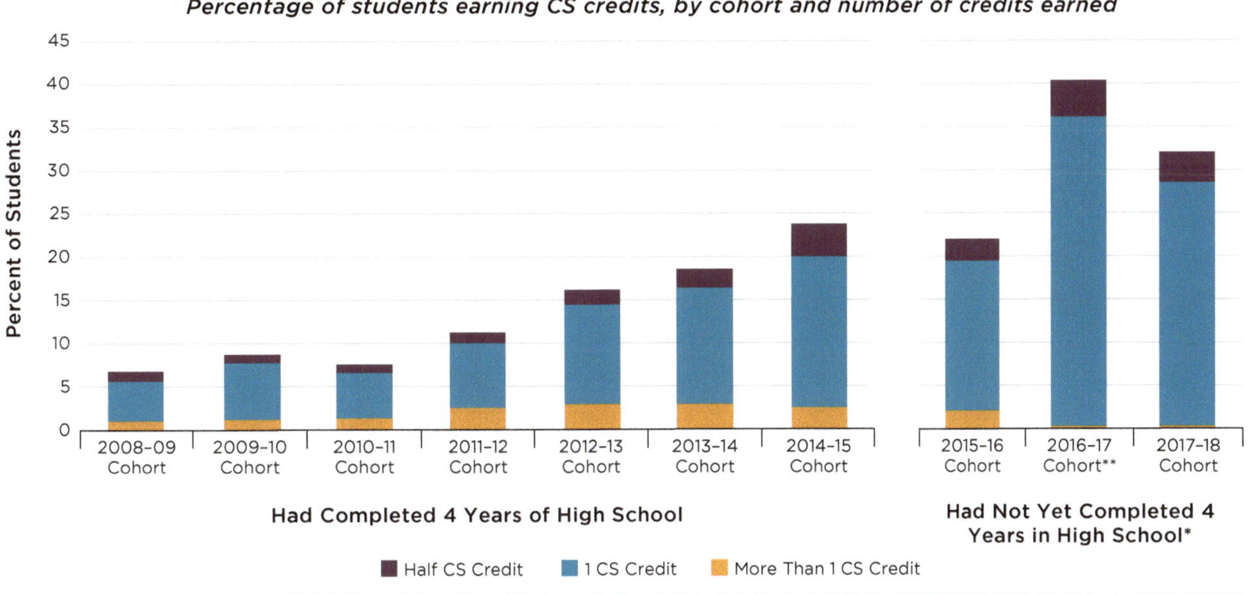

Note: Cohorts refer to ninth-grade cohort, labeled by the ninth-grade school year. Remaining students earned no CS credits. *Our study sample includes data from 2008-09 through 2017-18; we have 4 years of high school course data only for students through the 2014-15 cohort. **First cohort subject to the CS graduation requirement.

of the ECS curriculum in the 2012–13 school year (the 2012–13 to 2017–18 cohorts). For each cohort, we use regression analysis to compare students' GPAs in their core, CS, and elective courses, considering their grades over their first four years in high school (see Appendix C).[50]

Figure 14 displays regression-adjusted GPAs in core, CS, and elective courses for students in each cohort analyzed. Across cohorts, high school students earned higher average grades in their CS classes than in their core subjects. Average grades in CS courses ranged from around 2.6 grade points for the earliest cohort to around 2.8 grade points for the most recent cohort. Both CS and core GPAs trended up over time, but the difference between these two class types remained equal to about 0.2 grade points on average across cohorts.[51]

In contrast, average grades in elective courses were higher than average CS grades, although this difference is smaller. On average, students' elective course grades were 0.1 grade points higher than their CS grades. This

small difference disappeared for students in the last cohort, which we only observed during their first year of high school.

CS vs. Core Course Grades: Gender, Race/Ethnicity, SES

To examine differences between CS and core grades across student groups, we performed similar regression analysis using the same cohorts previously analyzed. Overall, we find that average CS grades exceeded average grades in core subjects for all student groups by roughly one-quarter of a grade-point.

Each bar in **Figure 15** represents the regression-adjusted difference between CS and core grade averages for each student group. The differences between average CS grades and average core course grades range from 0.22 grade points for Latino students to 0.27 grade points for White students. Overall, we find that the GPA differences were very similar across gender, race/ethnicity, and neighborhood SES.

---

50 For these analyses, elective courses are those that are neither core subjects (math, English, social studies, or science) nor CS. These include world language, business and vocational courses, art and music, and physical education, among others.

51 The only exception is the 2012-13 cohort, for which the grade-point difference between CS and core courses was 0.3.

Students Earned Higher Grades in CS Courses Than in Other Core Courses

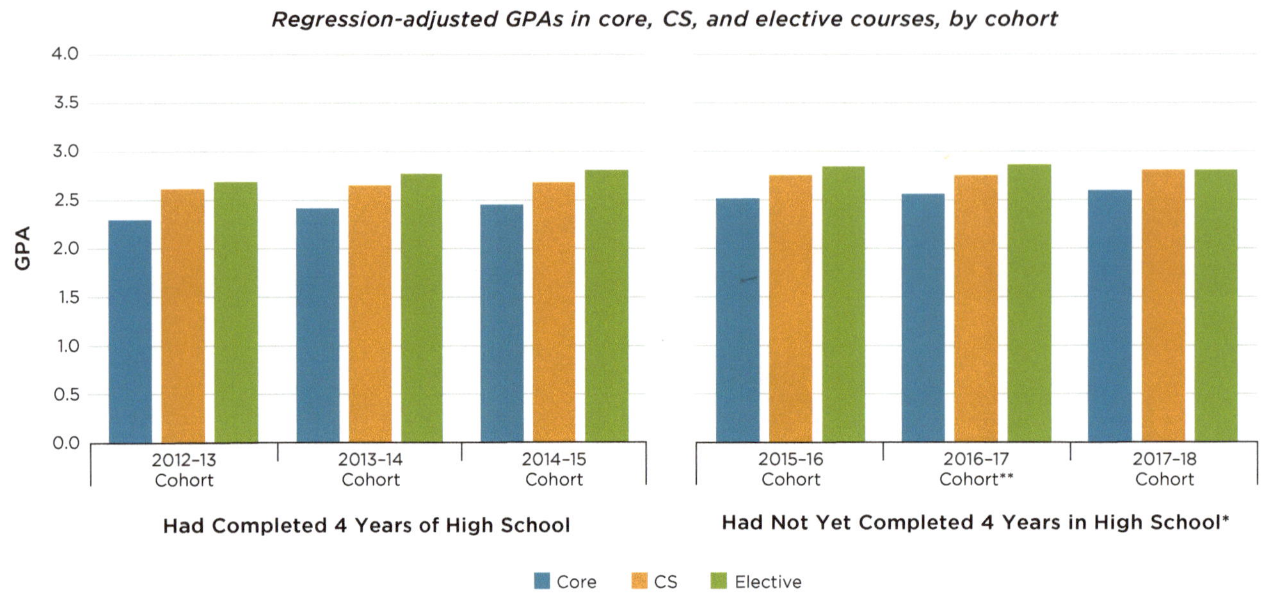

Note: Cohorts refer to ninth-grade cohort, labeled by the ninth-grade school year. *Our study sample includes data from 2008–09 through 2017–18; we have 4 years of high school course data only for students through the 2014–15 cohort. **First cohort subject to the CS graduation requirement.

Differences Between CS and Core Course Grades Were Similar Across Student Gender, Race/Ethnicity, and Neighborhood SES

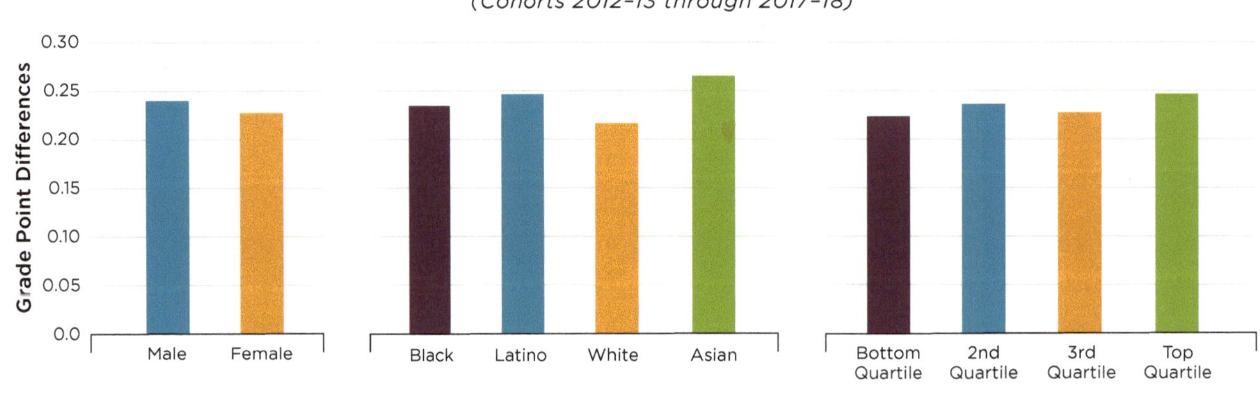

Note: Cohorts refer to ninth-grade cohort, labeled by the ninth-grade school year. Control variables include student, grade-level, and school fixed effects, and regressions were estimated separately for each student group considered. See Appendix Tables C.2–4 for more details.

Summary

Grades in CS courses were higher on average than core course grades and increased over time, despite increasing shares of students taking a CS course. CS grades exceeded grade averages in core subjects across all student groups by about one-quarter of a grade-point. Students from the most recent cohorts were earning one or more CS credits at higher rates; 36 percent of the 2016–17 cohort (the first subject to the graduation requirement) earned at least one credit in CS during the first two years of high school compared, with only 20 percent of the 2014–15 cohort over the first four years of high school.

CHAPTER 4

Interpretive Summary

Nationwide, states and school districts have adopted various initiatives aimed at increasing CS opportunities for all students in efforts to prepare them with the skills needed to fully participate in today's economy. CPS stands out as one of the first school districts implementing an initiative to bring a CS curriculum into every high school and the first to make CS a core graduation requirement, starting with the graduating class of 2020. Efforts to expand access to CS successfully raised the number of CPS high schools offering CS courses, as well as the number of students enrolling in such classes.

By 2018, more than 90 percent of students had access to at least one CS course in their school. About 80 percent of neighborhood and other citywide high schools and all selective enrollment high schools offered at least one CS course by 2018.[52] The 20 percent of high schools that were not yet offering a CS course in 2018 were smaller, on average, in terms of total student enrollment. Expanded access to CS was accompanied by increased enrollment in CS. However, the percentage of students who enrolled in any CS course remained below 30 percent for the student cohorts who graduated just before the graduation requirement took effect.

Enrollment rates for all student groups increased following the introduction of the CS4All initiative. After accounting for differences in access to CS courses using the 2014–15 cohort, Black students were somewhat more likely than the average student to enroll in a CS course, while Latino students were somewhat less likely than the average student to enroll in a CS course. For this same cohort, differences in enrollment rates by neighborhood SES virtually disappeared once we accounted for differences in access—students living in high and low-SES neighborhoods were equally likely to have enrolled in at least one CS course. In contrast,

male students remained more likely than female students to enroll in at least one CS course.

This study examined the expansion of CS courses in CPS high schools, changes to student enrollment in CS classes, and the performance of students in these classes during the school years 2008–09 to 2017–18. Our findings offer important considerations for CPS and other districts expanding their CS offerings:

Recruiting, training, and retaining skilled teachers may be one of the main challenges for districts to overcome in adopting similar policies. One of the primary objectives of the CS4All initiative was to expand CS access to every high school in CPS by 2019. While the district made considerable efforts to accomplish this goal, and CS offerings at the high school level rapidly expanded in CPS after the introduction of the CS4All initiative, 20 percent of high schools did not yet offer any CS courses in 2018, even though some currently-enrolled students were subject to the graduation requirement. CPS subsequently reported that all district-run high schools offered CS in the 2019–20 school year.

As many states across the country embark on the

---

52 CPS reports that all district-run high schools are offering CS in the 2019–20 school year. See CPS Office of Computer Science website, "Where Can My Child Take Computer Science" https://sites.google.com/cps. edu/cs4all/for-parents/where-can-my-child-take-cs

mission of expanding CS education opportunities for all students, one of the main barriers they commonly face is a shortage of CS teachers.[53] For instance, a 2016 Google-Gallup survey on K–12 trends in CS found that the most common reason reported by principals and superintendents for not offering CS was the lack of qualified teachers in their schools or funds to train them.[54] In 2017, there were only 100 teachers across the nation who graduated from a Title II teacher preparation institution certified to teach CS, in striking contrast to more than 10,000 graduating math teachers.[55] On the other hand, staffing CS teachers is not only an issue of finding graduates with the necessary skillset, but also of attracting and retaining qualified CS majors into the teaching profession when high-paying job opportunities grow every day in the computing and tech industry. This challenge is not unique to the elementary and secondary school level. Demand for CS courses by majors and non-majors at the undergraduate level has outstripped the supply of faculty in part due to a majority of new PhDs in computer science going into industry rather than academia.[56]

An alternative adopted by many school districts nationwide is to invest resources in teacher professional development and certification programs in computer science. For example, the widely-offered ECS curriculum provides a professional development program for teachers who want to teach this introductory-level CS course. However, teachers need rigorous certifications and credentials in order to teach higher-level CS courses, such as AP CS, although this varies by state. Districts and states will need more concrete plans to expand CS pre-service teacher programs and develop alternative CS teacher certification pathways in order to meet the increasing demand for teachers of higher-level CS courses.

Expanding access and enrollment in advanced CS classes may require additional strategies. Another aim of the CS4All initiative was to expand enrollment in AP CS classes with the hope of expanding interest in CS careers. To achieve this objective, a goal of CS4All was to offer AP CS classes in one-half of CPS high schools.

As of 2018, the share of CPS high schools offering AP CS courses was 18 percent, up from 6 percent in 2013. However, despite the increase in access to AP CS classes, the percentage of students enrolling in advanced CS courses (intermediate-level CS and AP CS) remained unchanged, at around 5 percent.

The goal of offering AP classes in more high schools faces similar challenges as the expansion of introductory classes—namely, recruiting, training, and retaining qualified teachers. Therefore, strategies to help high schools overcome these obstacles for introductory-level courses may also help with the more advanced CS courses. However, expanding enrollment in AP CS seems to be a bigger challenge than simply expanding access. Exposing more students to the introductory-level ECS course was intended, in part, to spark student interest in CS and make students more likely to enroll in higher-level courses. Nevertheless, increased exposure to ECS combined with greater access to AP CS has not led to increases in enrollment.

One potential strategy to help increase enrollment is a new AP CS class, AP CS Principles, introduced by the College Board in 2016–17. It, like ECS, is aimed at increasing the participation of students who are often underrepresented in CS. Nationwide, the number of AP test-takers in computer science has been slowly increasing since the introduction of AP CS Principles, as has the representation of female, Black, and Latino students in AP CS. In CPS, this course may help increase overall CS enrollment over the next few years. The share of female AP CS students in CPS has increased, and although still below one-half, it is close to one-third for the 2014–15 cohort. Asian and White students are still overrepresented in AP CS classes, however, relative to CPS as a whole.

Finally, the CS4All initiative in CPS also included plans to expand CS access to elementary grade students. In the longer run, expanding CS offerings in elementary schools may help increase student enrollment in higher-level CS courses while in high school, and subsequently increase the number of CPS graduates pursuing careers in CS.

53 Herold (2018, February 19); Google Inc., & Gallup Inc. (2016).
54 Google Inc., & Gallup Inc. (2016).
55 Title II (2018).
56 National Academies of Sciences, Engineering, and Medicine (2017).

 The ECS curriculum and corresponding PD program for teachers were designed to broaden the appeal of CS to student groups that have been underrepresented in CS. While differences in CS enrollment rates in CPS were reduced or eliminated for students with different races/ethnicities and SES after the ECS curriculum was adopted, differences in CS enrollment between male and female students were not reduced. Although enrollment rates for both male and female students increased after the introduction and expansion of ECS courses, the increase was faster for male students, whose enrollment rates were 9 percentage points higher than female students in the 2013–14 cohort. This was up from a difference of 4 percentage points in the 2010–11 cohort and 3 percentage points in the 2008–09 cohort. Among ninth-grade students in the 2017–18 cohort, the enrollment rate difference remained at 9 percentage points. These differences are not due to differences in access to CS courses, as female students are somewhat more likely than male students are to attend high schools offering at least one CS course. Instead, other factors such as societal narratives about who belongs in and succeeds within CS and/or limited female role models in the field may make enrolling CS courses less appealing to female students than enrolling in other courses.

While the graduation requirement will likely lead to at least a partial reduction of the difference in enrollment rates between male and female students, the fact that some students are eligible to receive waivers for the requirement means that gender differences could remain. Even if male and female students are equally likely to be eligible to receive a CS waiver, the fact that female students were less likely than male students to take CS when CS was an elective indicates that female students may be more likely to take advantage of the waiver rather than enroll in a CS course. Thus, districts may need additional strategies to attract and engage more female students into CS, and to reach similar enrollment rates among female and male students.

 Districts working to increase student enrollment in CS courses are doing so because they consider CS as essential as biology and other core subjects for students to thrive in the 21st century. Introducing CS as a graduation requirement has implications and tradeoffs for districts to consider.

One question for attention is: what tradeoffs are students, counselors, and administrators juggling as they create class schedules once CS graduation requirements take effect? In CPS, the CS requirement appears to be less flexible than the Career Education credit requirement that it replaced; a wider variety of courses satisfied the Career Education requirement than is true for the CS requirement.[57] For college-bound students encouraged to take more credits in math, science, social studies, and world language than the CPS graduation requirements, a CS course may be difficult to juggle in an already-crowded schedule.

A second consideration is what purpose a course waiver serves, and what effects it has on students. In CPS, some students will be eligible to waive the CS credit requirement. As a result, the CS graduation requirement may not lead to all CPS students gaining exposure to CS. At the same time, some students will not be eligible for a CS waiver and may find it difficult to meet the CS graduation requirement within four years. At the end of the 2017–18 school year, less than one-half (42%) of the students in the 2016–17 cohort—who are the first to graduate under the new CS requirement—had taken at least one CS course. If a large share of those not having taken a CS course are ineligible for a waiver, it may be difficult for schools to provide enough seats in CS courses to accommodate the remaining 2016–17 cohort students, in addition to students in the following cohorts who are also subject to the graduation requirement.

Students' course grades are a third area that may be affected when CS courses become required for graduation. In CPS, as CS offerings and enrollment expanded over the past five years, student CS grade averages have

---

57 See *Computer Science in CPS* on p.7 for more details.

remained high compared to their other core courses. CS courses had very low failure rates and, as shown in Chapter 3, CS course grades were higher, on average, than students' core course grades by roughly 0.2 grade points. Course grades in non-CS elective courses were also higher than grade averages in core courses. Students often enroll in electives based upon interest, which may influence motivation and ultimately success. As CS becomes required for all students, average interest and motivation may drop and grades may therefore also drop. Thus, early data on students' course grades in CS electives may not accurately predict CS course grades once CS becomes required. There is no early evidence of this in CPS for the 2016–17 and 2017–18 cohorts. But it is something that CPS and other districts adding CS graduation requirements may want to watch.

Conclusion

Computational thinking is applicable to a wide variety of careers and disciplines of study. Consequently, many within and outside of the CS and technology field believe CS skills are necessary to thrive in the future economy and that educators should expose students to CS, just as they expose students to math, biology, and English. As numerous districts across the nation are adding CS to their curriculum in both high school and elementary grade levels, this report provides a preliminary look at some of the successes and challenges in one district that has put considerable resources and political will behind an effort to increase CS education for all students. Chicago's efforts to increase exposure at all grade levels is ongoing, and we will begin to see the full impact of these efforts in the years to come.

References

Association for Computing Machinery (ACM). (2016)
K–12 computer science framework. Retrieved from
http://www.k12cs.org

Bureau of Labor Statistics. (2019)
Occupational outlook handbook. Retrieved from https://
www.bls.gov/ooh/computer-and-information-technology/
home.htm

Century, J., Lach, M., King, H., Rand, S., Heppner, C.,
Franke, B., & Westrick, J. (2013)
Building an operating system for computer science.
Retrieved from http://outlier.uchicago.edu/computer-
science/OS4CS/stories/chicago/

CPS Office of Computer Science. (n.d.)
Computer science waivers. Retrieved from https://sites.
google.com/cps.edu/cs4all/for-administrators/cs-waivers

CPS Office of Teaching and Learning. (2019)
High school course catalog. Retrieved from https://cps.edu/
SiteCollectionDocuments/HighSchoolCourseCatalog.pdf

Code.org Advocacy Coalition. (2019)
*2019 state of computer science education: Equity and
diversity.* Retrieved from https://advocacy.code.org/2019_
state_of_cs.pdf

Dettori, L., Greenburg, R.I., McGee, S., & Reed, D. (2016)
The impact of the exploring computer science instruction-
al model in Chicago Public Schools. *Computing in Science
& Engineering, 18*(2), 1–8.

Elahi, A. (2016, March 1)
CPS to roll out computer science requirement. *Chicago
Tribune.* Chicago, IL. Retrieved from http://www.chicago-
tribune.com/bluesky/originals/ct-computer-science-gradu-
ation-cps-bsi-20160225-story.html

Fayer, S., Lacey, A., & Watson, A. (2017)
*BLS spotlight on statistics: STEM occupations – past,
present, and future.* Washington, DC: U.S. Department of
Labor, Bureau of Labor Statistics.

Goode, J., & Margolis, J. (2011)
Exploring computer science: A case study of school reform.
ACM Transactions on Computing Education, 11(2), 1–16.

Google Inc., & Gallup Inc. (2015)
*Images of computer science: Perceptions among students,
parents and educators in the U.S.* Retrieved from https://
www.google.com/edu/resources/computerscience/research/

Google Inc., & Gallup Inc. (2016)
Trends in the state of computer science in U.S. K–12 schools.
Retrieved from http://goo.gl/j291E0

Google Inc., & Gallup Inc. (2017)
K–12 computer science education state reports. Retrieved
from http://goo.gl/wzALQK

Heitin, L. (2016, January 30)
President Obama announces 'Computer Science For All'
initiative. *Education Week.* Retrieved from http://blogs.
edweek.org/edweek/curriculum/2016/01/white_house_
computer_science_for_all_initiative.html

Herold, B. (2018, February 19)
Computer science for all: Can schools pull it off?.
Education Week. Retrieved from https://www.edweek.org/
ew/articles/2018/02/20/computer-science-for-all-can-
schools-pull.html

Margolis, J., Ryoo, J.J., Sandoval, C.D.M., Lee, C., Goode, J.,
& Chapman, G. (2012)
Beyond access: Broadening participation in high school
computer science. *ACM Inroads, 3*(4), 72–78.

McGee, S., McGee-Tekula, R., Duck, J., Dettori, L., Yanek, D.,
Rasmussen, A.M., Greenberg, R.I., & Reed, D.F. (2018, April 14)
Does exploring computer science increase computer
science enrollment? Paper presented at American
Educational Research Association's *The Dreams,
Possibilities, and Necessity of Public Education* annual
conference, New York, NY.

McGee, S., McGee-Tekula, R., Duck, J., Greenberg,
R., Dettori, L., Reed, D.F., Wilkerson, B., Yanek, D.,
Rasmussen, A.M., & Chapman, G. (2017)
Does a taste of computing increase computer science
enrollment? Computing in Science & Engineering.
Special Issue: Best of RESPECT 2016, 19(3), 8–18.

National Academies of Sciences, Engineering, and
Medicine. (2017)
*Assessing and responding to the growth of computer
science undergraduate enrollments.* Washington, DC:
The National Academies Press. Retrieved from
https://doi.org/10.17226/24926

National Center of Education Statistics (NCES). (2018)
Digest of Education Statistics. Table 219.30. Public high
school graduates, by race/ethnicity: 1989–90 through
2028–29. Retrieved from https://nces.ed.gov/programs/
digest/d18/tables/dt18_219.30.asp

Papanno, L. (2017, April 4)
Learning to think like a computer. *New York Times.*
Retrieved from https://www.nytimes.com/2017/04/04/
education/edlife/teaching-students-computer-code.html

Reed, D., Wilkerson, B., Yanek, D., Dettori, L., & Solin, J. (2015)
How Exploring Computer Science (ECS) came to Chicago. *ACM Inroads, 6*(3), 75–77.

Scott, A., Koshy, S., Rao, M., Hinton, L., Flapan, J., Martin, A., & McAlear, F. (2019)
Computer science in California's schools: Access, enrollment and equity. Oakland, CA: Kapor Center.

Snyder, T.D., de Brey, C., & Dillow, S.A. (2019)
Digest of education statistics 2017 (53rd Ed.). Washington, DC: National Center for Education Statistics. Retrieved from https://nces.ed.gov/programs/digest/2017menu_tables.asp

The College Board. (2019)
AP program participation and performance data 2019. Retrieved from https://research.collegeboard.org/programs/ap/data

Title II. (2018)
Higher education act reports: National teacher preparation data. Retrieved from https://title2.ed.gov/Public/Report/DataFiles/DataFiles.aspx?p=5_01

Tucker, A., McCowan, D., Deek, F., Stephenson, C., Jones, J., & Verno, A. (2006)
A model curriculum for K–12 computer science: Report of the ACM K–12 Task Force Computer Science Curriculum Committee (2nd Ed.). New York, NY: Association for Computing Machinery.

Wing, J.M. (2006)
Computational thinking. *Communication of the ACM, 49*(3), 33–35.

Yadav, A., Gretter, S., Hambrusch, S.E., & Sands, P. (2016)
Expanding computer science education in schools: understanding teacher experiences and challenges. *Computer Science Education, 26*(4), 235–254.

Zumbach, L. (2013, December 10)
CPS making computer science core subject. *Chicago Tribune.* Retrieved from http://articles.chicagotribune.com/2013-12-10/news/ct-cps-computer-science-plan-met-1210-20131210_1_computer-science-ceo-barbara-byrd-bennett-code-org

Appendix A
Data and Sample Demographics

This study relies on administrative data from CPS, including students' enrollment records, background information, standardized test scores from middle school, and high school grades and transcripts.

A. Enrollment Records: Masterfile data provide enrollment information for all active students over the period studied, including those who are enrolled in a charter or non-traditional high school. Although we get information about students' grade-level from the Masterfile data, when there were discrepancies between the fall and spring grade-level reported we used the Attribute files, which provide the annualized grade-level of students. This allowed us to identify the grade in which students were enrolled at the end of the school year.

B. Background Information: Masterfile data also provide information on student demographics (race/ethnicity, gender), free or reduced-price lunch status, special education status, and residential neighborhood. We also use a Consortium measure of poverty concentration that corresponds to students' neighborhoods based on census data.

C. Standardized Test Scores: We use students' eighth-grade math test scores (ISAT or NWEA, depending on the cohort) and standardize the scores within school year to have a mean of 0 and a standard deviation of 1. For this, we included all students enrolled in CPS in a given year, including students who ultimately were not part of our study sample. Our study sample performed slightly better than the district average (**see Table A.2**).

D. High School Grades and Transcripts: High school grade files contain information on student course enrollment for up to 22 courses per student. Records include the course title and number; course level; section number; semester of enrollment; mid-term and final grades; and a teacher identification code. These data also include a unique school code which we use to identify the high school in which a student is taking courses and earning credits. We also use this school as the high school in which a student is enrolled.[58]

E. Geographical Regions in the City of Chicago: We used geographical information from the City of Chicago Data Portal to map the 77 different community areas in the city. Community areas were grouped into regions or "sides", as follows:

Far North Side: 01, 02, 03, 04, 09, 10, 11, 12, 13, 14, 76, 77
Northwest Side: 15, 16, 17, 18, 19, 20
North Side: 05, 06, 07, 21, 22
West Side: 23, 24, 25, 26, 27, 28, 29, 30, 31
Central Side: 08, 32 and 33
Southwest Side: 56, 57, 58, 59, 61, 62, 63, 64, 65, 66, 67, 68
South Side: 34, 35, 36, 37, 38, 39, 40, 41, 42, 43, 60, 69
Far Southwest Side: 70, 71, 72, 73, 74, 75.
Far Southeast Side: 44, 45, 46, 47, 48, 49, 50, 51, 52, 53, 54, 55 [59]

FIGURE A.1

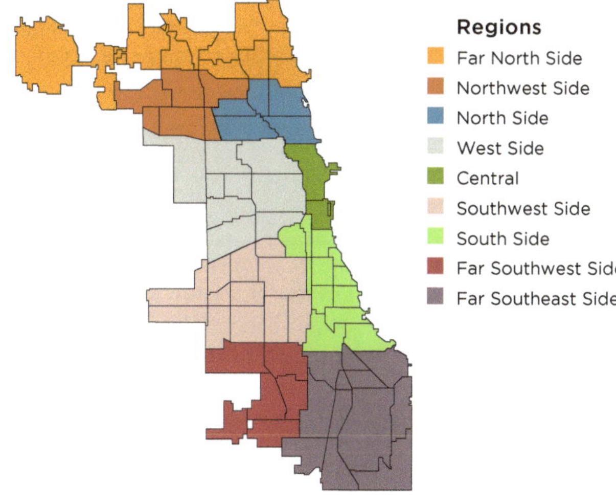

---

58 There are some discrepancies between the Masterfile data and the grade file data regarding the school enrolled. This arises in part because students may change schools between the date when the Masterfile data are pulled from CPS records and the end of the semester.

59 Source: https://www.chicagohealthatlas.org/community-areas

CS Courses in This Study

The CPS Office of Computer Science provided us with course code numbers and the high school course catalog in order to identify CS courses from students' grade file data. In addition, the office provided course codes for introductory-level CS courses following the implementation of the ECS curriculum. This allowed us to differentiate introductory-level CS courses, those that follow the ECS curriculum, from more advanced course-offerings such as robotics, IT problem solving, programming, and AP CS.[60]

In some cases, courses were computer-related but not considered CS. For example, courses such as information technology, digital media, graphic design and communication, keyboarding or typewriting were computer related courses but were not CS. It is also the case that when the ECS curriculum was first introduced, some courses identified as Fundamentals of Information Technology (FIT) were using the ECS curriculum, and therefore considered CS, while others were not. In order to identify which FIT courses were considered ECS, we identified whether the course teacher had received training in the ECS curriculum, using CS professional development rosters and personnel data provided by CPS.

Courses considered CS for this study included those that presented basic CS concepts considered foundational for understanding more advanced CS topics (primarily, introductory-level CS following the ECS curriculum), as well as more specialized courses that focused on specific programming languages and CS-related topics such as robotics (intermediate-level CS) and AP CS. Although all the CS courses included in this study were identified by the Office of Computer Science as such, some were not eligible for the CS graduation requirement according to the most recent CPS High School Course Catalog (e.g., Gaming Concepts, Relational Databases, Java and Media Computation, Digital Computation Systems, and Advanced Data Structures).

The introduction of the CS4All initiative brought more clarity about which courses were considered CS in CPS. **Table A.1** presents examples of some of the most common CS courses that are offered in CPS high schools.

TABLE A.1

Common CS Course Titles in CPS

Course Titles	Brief Description[62]	Graduation Credit	Prerequisites/ Level
Exploring Computer Science	Exploring Computer Science is a nationally recognized introductory college preparatory computer science course (…) ECS is composed of six foundational units with lessons that are designed to promote an inquiry-based approach to teaching and learning foundational concepts in computer science and highlighting the computational practices and problem solving associated with doing computer science. **CTE Program:** Computer Science for All (CSA)	Computer Science; Career Ed; Elective	None/ Introductory-Level
STEM Intro Computer Science; Taste of Computing	The course units draw on the curricular framework listed in Levels II and III of the ACM's A Model Curriculum for K–12 Computer Science (2003). Assignments and instruction are contextualized to be socially relevant and meaningful for diverse students. Units utilize a variety of tools/platforms and culminate with final projects around the following topics: Human Computer Interaction, Problem Solving, Web Design, Programming, Computing and Data Analysis, and Robotics. **CTE Program:** IT STEM Orientation	Computer Science; Career Ed; Elective	None/ Introductory-Level

---

60 All introductory-level CS courses were using the ECS curriculum except a *Computer Science* course offered at one high school. The introductory CS courses that were also considered ECS were: Exploring Computer Science, Taste of Computing, Exploring Computational Thinking, Intro to Computer Science STEM/STEM IT Introduction to Computer Science, and Fundamentals of Information Technology (whenever the teacher was ECS trained).

62 Retrieved from the CPS Office of Teaching and Learning (2019).

Course Title	Brief Description	Graduation Credit	Prerequisites/ Level
Fundamentals of IT	This is the first course in a three-year sequence of all Information technology classes. The primary purpose of this course is to introduce students to the breadth of the field of computer science through an exploration of engaging and accessible topics. Focused on the conceptual ideas if computing, it helps students understand why certain tools or languages might be utilized to solve particular problems. The goal is to develop the computational thinking practices of algorithm development, problem solving and programming within the context of problems that are relevant to the lives of today's students. They will also be introduced to interface design, limits of computers and societal and ethical issues. (...) **CTE Program:** IT Orientation (regular level); IT STEM Orientation (honors level)	Computer Science; Career Ed; Elective	None/ Introductory-Level
AP Computer Science Principles	The AP Computer Science Principles course is designed to be equivalent to a first-semester introductory college computing course. In this course students will develop computational thinking vital for success across all disciplines, such as computational tools to analyze and study data and working with large data sets to analyze visualize, and draw conclusions from trends. Students are encouraged to apply creative processes when developing computational artifacts and to think creatively while using computer software and other technology to explore questions that interest them. Students will develop communication and collaboration skills, working individual and collaboratively to solve problems.	Computer Science; Career Ed; Elective	Algebra I *Teacher certification at AP summer institute required Advanced/ AP-Level
AP Computer Science A	The AP Computer Science A course is an introductory course in computer science. Because the design and implementation of computer programs to solve problems involve skills that are fundamental to the study of computer science, a large part of the course is built around the development of computer programs that correctly solve a given problem. These programs should be understandable, adaptable, and, when appropriate, reusable. At the same time, the design and implementation of computer programs is used as a context for introducing other important aspects of computer science, including the development and analysis of algorithms, the development and use of fundamental data structures, the study of standard algorithms and typical applications, and the use of logic and formal methods.	Computer Science; Career Ed; Elective	Algebra, Algebra II and Trigonometry, and Geometry *Teacher certification at AP summer institute required Advanced/ AP-Level
IT Problem Solving	This course will give students hands-on experience in a wide range of modern information technology. Several IT concepts will be introduced that will provide a basis for further study in Information Technology. Students will work on a number of projects that will give perspectives on areas of IT including but not limited to: visual and/or robotic programming, social networking tools, web design and networking. Issues of security, privacy and ethics will also be examined. Students will leave the course with an understanding of the components of modern IT systems and the scope of knowledge needed to become an IT professional. **CTE Program:** IT STEM Orientation	Computer Science; Career Ed; Elective	None/ Intermediate-Level

Course Title	Brief Description	Graduation Credit	Prerequisites/ Level
Introduction to Robotics	Introduction to Robotics is a course designed to introduce students to the branch of technology that deals with the design, construction, operation, and application of robotic mechanisms. Students will explore various applications of STEM through computer programming, 3D design drafting, applied physics and mathematics as well as robot construction. This course will include hands-on activities and team projects. Students will be able to design, build and program robots that use a variety of sensors to interact with the environment. Students will use robotics to design and propose a solution to a challenging, real-world problem.	Computer Science; Career Ed; Elective	None/ Intermediate-Level
Programming	Students will learn the fundamentals of Object Oriented Programming. Using Ruby, they'll learn to analyze problems, think algorithmically about logic and design, and build/debug programs that accept input and return output while using variables, operators, data types, methods, arguments, blocks, control structures, and classes.	Computer Science; Career Ed; Elective	None/ Intermediate-Level

TABLE A.2

Number of Students and Schools Included in the Study, by School Year

	2008–09	2009–10	2010–11	2011–12	2012–13	2013–14	2014–15	2015–16	2016–17	2017–18
Students	95,312	93,833	88,925	86,391	83,803	80,052	77,817	75,961	73,942	73,375
Percent of Total HS Enrollment	84%	81%	78%	76%	75%	71%	69%	68%	68%	68%
Schools	93	96	98	92	93	95	93	91	90	90

TABLE A.3

Demographic Characteristics of Each Study Cohort

	2008–09 Cohort Class of 2012	2009–10 Cohort Class of 2013	2010–11 Cohort Class of 2014	2011–12 Cohort Class of 2015	2012–13 Cohort Class of 2016	2013–14 Cohort Class of 2017	2014–15 Cohort Class of 2018	2015–16 Cohort Class of 2019	2016–17 Cohort Class of 2020	2017–18 Cohort Class of 2021
Total Number of Students	27,247	25,297	23,546	23,115	22,164	21,492	21,629	20,510	19,541	19,386
% Female	51.0	51.5	50.7	51.6	51.0	51.8	51.3	50.8	51.0	50.4
% Asian	4.0	4.4	4.4	4.7	4.5	4.9	4.8	5.2	5.3	5.1
% Black	47.2	42.4	39.8	38.1	36.8	35.5	34.5	33.0	32.7	31.8
% Latino	39.7	42.9	44.9	45.6	47.3	47.4	48.2	49.0	48.7	49.7
% White	8.3	8.9	9.3	9.9	9.8	10.6	10.9	11.0	11.6	11.1
% Free/ Reduced-Price Lunch	84.8	84.7	84.2	84.4	84.0	83.3	82.3	81.4	80.0	79.4
% Special Ed	13.8	13.4	13.7	13.5	13.6	13.3	13.2	13.3	14.1	14.3
% Graduated in 4 Years	75.3	77.8	80.7	81.8	82.0	83.5	84.2	—	—	—

Ninth-Grade Cohorts Used for Analyses and Figures

Cohort	Cumulative CS Enrollment	Enrollment Differences, by Student Characteristics	CS classes Composition, by Student Demographics	Regression-Adjusted Enrollment Differences, by Student Characteristics	CS Credits Earned Over First Four Years in HS	Regression-Adjusted GPAs in Core, CS, & Elective Courses	Regression-Adjusted Differences Between Core & CS GPAs, by Student Groups
	Figure 5	Figures 6–8	Table 2	Figures 9–11	Figure 13	Figure 14	Figure 15
2008–09 Class of 2012	X	X		X	X		
2009–10 Class of 2013	X	X			X		
2010–11 Class of 2014	X	X	X		X		
2011–12 Class of 2015	X	X			X		
2012–13 Class of 2016	X	X			X	X	X
2013–14 Class of 2017	X	X			X	X	X
2014–15 Class of 2018	X	X	X	X	X	X	X
2015–16 Class of 2019	X				X	X	X
2016–17 Class of 2020	X				X	X	X
2017–18 Class of 2021	X				X	X	X

Appendix B
Enrollment Differences

Using regression analyses on a sample of students in the 2014–15 cohort who were enrolled in a high school that offered at least one CS course over their first four years of high school, we assessed how enrolling in at least one CS course was related to students' gender, race/ethnicity, and neighborhood SES, while also including an indicator for the number of years—one to four—that a student was enrolled in a high school that offered at least one CS course.

The dependent variable in the regression model is the difference between the indicator for an individual student enrolling in at least one CS course and the over-all average enrollment rate for the sample of students who were enrolled at least one year in a high school that offered CS. Models 1 through 3 estimate the overall enrollment rate difference between the average student and that particular student group. Model 4 estimates these same enrollment rate differences when we only consider students who were enrolled in a school that offered at least one CS course during a student's first four years of high school. Additionally, it accounts for the number of years enrolled in a school offering CS and student demographic characteristics (i.e. gender, race/ethnicity, and neighborhood SES quartile).

TABLE B.1

Predicted CS Enrollment Rates, Unadjusted and Conditional on Access, Cohort 2014–15

VARIABLES	(1)	(2)	(3)	(4)
Female	-0.0901*** (0.00588)			-0.119*** (0.00656)
Black		-0.0179* (0.0104)		0.0754*** (0.0128)
Latino		-0.0126 (0.0102)		0.00841 (0.0114)
Asian		0.0755*** (0.0169)		0.0475*** (0.0179)
Other		0.0121 (0.0247)		0.0363 (0.0267)
2nd SES Quartile			0.0299*** (0.00832)	0.00506 (0.0101)
3rd SES Quartile			0.0496*** (0.00831)	0.0145 (0.0105)
Top SES Quartile			0.0355*** (0.00829)	0.000867 (0.0108)
2 Years of Access to CS				0.0271** (0.0110)
3 Years of Access to CS				0.126*** (0.0118)
4 Years of Access to CS				0.187*** (0.00896)
Constant	0.0456*** (0.00418)	0.00902 (0.00924)	-0.0283*** (0.00580)	-0.0938*** (0.0157)
Observations	21,629	21,629	21,606	18,530
R-Squared	0.011	0.002	0.002	0.047

Note: Models 1 through 3 predict the unadjusted CS enrollment difference by gender (1), race/ethnicity (2), and neighborhood SES (3). Model 4 predicts CS enrollment rates conditional on having access to CS and adjusting for years of access to CS and student demographic characteristics (gender, race/ethnicity, and neighborhood SES). Standard errors in parentheses; *** p<0.01, ** p<0.05, * p<0.1.

Appendix C
Regression Models Predicting CS, Electives, and Core GPAs

We used regression analyses on the sub-sample of students who took at least one CS class to compare their average GPA in CS to their average GPA in core subject courses (i.e., math, English, social studies, and science) taken during the same school year. The models include student fixed effects, which allow us to compare GPAs across subjects for the same student, while accounting for other factors that may be related to their academic performance in a particular school year. Models also control for grade-level and school fixed effects to account for differences across grade-levels and schools in which the students were enrolled.

We also explored whether there were differences in CS performance by gender (**Table C.2**), race/ethnicity (**Table C.3**), or neighborhood SES (**Table C.4**) and compared those to any differences we observed in core subjects. Regressions were estimated separately for each student group considered, and the models also included student, grade-level, and school fixed effects.

Adjusted Core, CS, and Electives GPAs, by Cohort

VARIABLES	Cohort 2012–13	Cohort 2013–14	Cohort 2014–15	Cohort 2015–16	Cohort 2016–17	Cohort 2017–18
CS Course	0.281*** (0.0102)	0.229*** (0.00998)	0.228*** (0.00917)	0.242*** (0.00978)	0.202*** (0.00776)	0.219*** (0.00905)
Elective	0.352*** (0.00230)	0.352*** (0.00229)	0.350*** (0.00227)	0.327*** (0.00253)	0.308*** (0.00298)	0.284*** (0.00395)
10th Grade	-0.173*** (0.00304)	-0.115*** (0.00307)	-0.0938*** (0.00304)	-0.123*** (0.00299)	-0.125*** (0.00290)	—
11th Grade	-0.176*** (0.00322)	-0.113*** (0.00321)	-0.153*** (0.00318)	-0.156*** (0.00313)	—	—
12th Grade	-0.129*** (0.00331)	-0.104*** (0.00330)	-0.140*** (0.00328)	—	—	—
School Fixed Effects	Yes	Yes	Yes	Yes	Yes	Yes
Student Fixed Effects	Yes	Yes	Yes	Yes	Yes	Yes
Constant	2.700*** (0.119)	2.489*** (0.0979)	3.178*** (0.0769)	3.027*** (0.148)	2.898*** (0.362)	3.233*** (0.293)
Observations	533,813	517,511	521,664	388,667	262,984	138,811
R-Squared	0.587	0.581	0.577	0.607	0.644	0.697

Note: Standard errors in parentheses; *** $p<0.01$, ** $p<0.05$, * $p<0.1$. Omitted category is core courses.

Adjusted CS and Core GPAs, by Gender

VARIABLES	Male GPA	Female GPA
CS	0.243*** (0.00517)	0.229*** (0.00585)
Elective	0.357*** (0.00155)	0.324*** (0.00143)
10th Grade	-0.139*** (0.00198)	-0.114*** (0.00184)
11th Grade	-0.179*** (0.00227)	-0.123*** (0.00208)
12th Grade	-0.190*** (0.00261)	-0.0635*** (0.00236)
School Fixed Eff cts	Yes	Yes
Student Fixed Eff cts	Yes	Yes
Constant	2.700*** (0.119)	2.489*** (0.0979)
Observations	1,153,754	1,209,696
R-Squared	0.599	0.579

Note: Standard errors in parentheses; *** p<0.01, ** p<0.05, * p<0.1 Omitted category is core courses.

Adjusted CS and Core GPAs, by Race/Ethnicity

VARIABLES	White GPA	Black GPA	Latino GPA	Asian GPA
CS	0.268*** (0.0101)	0.247*** (0.00673)	0.218*** (0.00581)	0.235*** (0.0131)
Elective	0.293*** (0.00280)	0.306*** (0.00184)	0.379*** (0.00156)	0.287*** (0.00396)
10th Grade	-0.0963*** (0.00357)	-0.119*** (0.00237)	-0.143*** (0.00198)	-0.0845*** (0.00503)
11th Grade	-0.0979*** (0.00401)	-0.112*** (0.00274)	-0.189*** (0.00225)	-0.147*** (0.00561)
12th Grade	-0.100*** (0.00453)	-0.0465*** (0.00314)	-0.173*** (0.00258)	-0.202*** (0.00632)
School Fixed Eff cts	Yes	Yes	Yes	Yes
Student Fixed Eff cts	Yes	Yes	Yes	Yes
Constant	3.697*** (0.691)	2.574*** (0.0488)	3.661*** (0.328)	4.763*** (0.277)
Observations	250,662	823,256	1,134,989	114,349
R-Squared	0.639	0.553	0.586	0.598

Note: Standard errors in parentheses; *** p<0.01, ** p<0.05, * p<0.1. Omitted category is core courses.

Adjusted CS and Core GPAs, by Neighborhood SES

VARIABLES	Bottom SES Quartile GPA	2nd SES Quartile GPA	3rd SES Quartile GPA	Top SES Quartile GPA
CS	0.247*** (0.00711)	0.228*** (0.00748)	0.238*** (0.00780)	0.225*** (0.00826)
Elective	0.352*** (0.00198)	0.364*** (0.00208)	0.342*** (0.00212)	0.304*** (0.00217)
10th Grade	-0.110*** (0.00264)	-0.125*** (0.00284)	-0.130*** (0.00294)	-0.144*** (0.00294)
11th Grade	-0.127*** (0.00308)	-0.165*** (0.00340)	-0.159*** (0.00353)	-0.157*** (0.00347)
12th Grade	-0.125*** (0.00353)	-0.155*** (0.00392)	-0.149*** (0.00409)	-0.0973*** (0.00402)
School Fixed Effects	Yes	Yes	Yes	Yes
Student Fixed Effects	Yes	Yes	Yes	Yes
Constant	3.634*** (0.248)	2.184*** (0.582)	3.092*** (0.130)	2.519*** (0.0590)
Observations	586,753	590,321	589,044	593,743
R-Squared	0.643	0.619	0.607	0.569

Note: Standard errors in parentheses; *** p<0.01, ** p<0.05, * p<0.1. Omitted category is core courses.

ABOUT THE AUTHORS

LISA BARROW is an Affiliated Researcher at the UChicago Consortium and a Senior Economist and Research Advisor at the Federal Reserve Bank of Chicago. Her research primarily focuses on policies and programs that have the potential to improve outcomes for low-income and otherwise less-advantaged individuals. She has worked in partnership with the UChicago Consortium studying the high school application process and the effectiveness of selective enrollment high schools. In other work, her research has used randomized evaluation to study whether computer-aided instruction can improve pre-algebra and algebra skills for students in larger urban school districts and whether performance-based scholarships can increase persistence and credit attainment among low-income community college students. Lisa received a PhD in economics from Princeton University.

SILVANA FREIRE is a Research Analyst at the UChicago Consortium. In this role, she conducts quantitative research to learn more about the experiences of CPS students and to identify relevant factors that play a key role in students' academic success and equitable learning opportunities. Before joining the UChicago Consortium, Silvana worked as a Research Assistant at the Graduate School of Education at Stanford University, while she was getting her master's degree in international education policy analysis.

MARISA DE LA TORRE is a Senior Research Associate and Managing Director at the UChicago Consortium. Her research interests include urban school reform, school choice, early indicators of school success, and English Learners. Before joining the UChicago Consortium, de la Torre worked for the Chicago Public Schools in the Office of Research, Evaluation, and Accountability. She received a master's degree in economics from Northwestern University.

THE FEDERAL RESERVE BANK OF CHICAGO is one of 12 regional Reserve Banks that, along with the Board of Governors in Washington, DC, make up the nation's central bank. The Chicago Reserve Bank serves the seventh Federal Reserve District, which encompasses the northern portions of Illinois and Indiana, southern Wisconsin, the Lower Peninsula of Michigan, and the state of Iowa. In addition to participation in the formulation of monetary policy, each Reserve Bank supervises member banks and bank holding companies, provides financial services to depository institutions and the U.S. government, and monitors economic conditions in its District.

FEDERAL RESERVE BANK OF CHICAGO

THE UNIVERSITY OF CHICAGO CONSORTIUM ON SCHOOL RESEARCH conducts research of high technical quality that can inform and assess policy and practice in the Chicago Public Schools. We seek to expand communication among researchers, policymakers, and practitioners as we support the search for solutions to the problems of school reform. The UChicago Consortium encourages the use of research in policy action and improvement of practice, but does not argue for particular policies or programs. Rather, we help to build capacity for school reform by identifying what matters for student success and school improvement, creating critical indicators to chart progress, and conducting theory-driven evaluation to identify how programs and policies are working. The UChicago Consortium is a unit of the Urban Education Institute.

This report reflects the interpretation of the authors. Although the UChicago Consortium's Steering Committee provided technical advice, no formal endorsement by these individuals, organizations, the full Consortium, the Federal Reserve Bank of Chicago, or the Federal Reserve System should be assumed.

9 780999 550977